Gee! I Wish I Had A Bedroom That Was All My Own

An Education Adventure In Interior Environment

by Michael Greene

"Gee! I Wish I Had a Bedroom That Was All My Own"
Copyright © 1995 by Michael Greene
All Rights Reserved
Design and layout by Michael Greene

Published By:
Tuesday's Child Publishing Ltd.
619B Heritage Hills
Somers, New York 10589

Library of Congress Catalog Card Number
Greene, Michael
97-090849

ISBN 1-881134-03-2

"Gee! I Wish I Had a Bedroom That Was All My Own"
Designed by Michael Greene
Character ink drawings by Rose Kennedy
Layout by Suki Koczeniak and Rolf Krauss

1. Home Furnishings 2. Interior Environment 3. Wood/Mica Furniture 4. Upholstery 5. Trees and Cotton 6. Education 7. Careers
8. Job Opportunities 9. Sleep Surfaces 10. Computer Design and Manufacturing (CAD) (CAM) 11. Spatial Relationships
12. Room Planning 13. Consumer Relationships 14. Selling (Retail and Manufacturing) 15. Marketing 16. Feng Shui 17. Thomas Day

First Edition
10 9 8 7 5 4 3 2 1

From Seed to Tree to Furniture

Wood furniture does not grow on trees. It is created in a partnership of nature and man.

Like all plant life: soil blend, moisture balance and climatic conditions determine the quality of the wood species. Fine wood furniture is created when knowledgeable forest growers and suppliers, designers, manufacturers and finishing specialists team up to provide the best in aesthetics, function and construction.

Generating mass-produced furniture for millions of people at a fair market price is an art form.

Armoire....
- A. Two doors with center inserts.
- B. Top pediment is pierced
- C. Two drawers in base.
- D. Interior designed with shirt compartment and five drawers.

Who Is Grandpa Mike?

He is Michael Greene.

And who is Michael Greene?

A real Grandpa weighing 124 pounds, with a lot of gray hair, plenty of arthritis, three children, ages forty to fifty and six grandchildren, ages nine to twenty five. Thanks to the Almighty, he has been married for fifty-three years to Grandma Anita and they have known one another for more than sixty years. She was his Number One girl and still is.

Michael is a regular columnist for two business newspapers: Furniture/Today, in Greensboro, North Carolina, covering the home furnishings industry and Home Textiles Today, in New York City, covering the home textile industry. Both newspapers are Cahners Business Newspapers, a division of Reed-Elsevier, Great Britain, published weekly, with readership throughout the world.

His columns have been translated in German in Switzerland and in Chinese in Taipei and Beijing. His Chinese name is Ling Ling. He has been chosen a member of the Writer's Hall of Fame of the furniture industry and an Honorary Member of IHFRA, the International Home Furnishings Representative Association.

He also writes a series called "On-The-Road with Michael Greene" in which he and Grandma visit with retail families in the home furnishings industry, all over North America, that usually have been in business for two or three generations. He has also written on interior environment for Newsday, Upholstery and Stores Magazines and Professional Furniture Merchant.

Michael has planned over twenty thousand children's rooms using mass produced factory furniture. He is the author of a children's illustrated book ("Where's The Green Pea?"); a composer and lyricist. He has conducted educational programs, with Grandma, in early childhood centers and public and private schools, using his book and music. Three new books are now being readied for printing.

Grandpa has presented seminars on phases of interior environment for the Fashion Institute of Technology, High Point University, the National Home Furnishings Association, manufacturers and retailers. He has done retail consulting projects for Olin Chemical, DeSoto Industries, Georgia-Pacific, Ethan Allen and Bramson Bedspread Manufacturing.

To round things out, Grandma and Grandpa do musical programs for senior citizens...like themselves.

Thanks, again, for listening.

From Grandpa Mike to readers

I am delighted to present, "Gee! I Wish I Had a Bedroom That Was All My Own – An Education Adventure in Interior Environment." I hope it will be your delight too.

The book is for middle school students and also for parents who might agree that it's not "kid stuff." It's a simple scenario of two youngsters and an "old-fashioned" grandpa with "old-fashioned" ideas, like earning before spending and telling others that you love them when you do.

Dovetailed in between is the panorama of interior environment that we all live in twenty four hours a day. During those twenty four hours we seem to take very little note of its creativity, its beauty and the opportunities it offers young people to express themselves. Honest.

Also, sandwiched between the lines is my belief that there is no "generation gap" except for the one that self-serving individuals create. I know because I am seventy-seven years old, thanks to the Almighty, and have spanned those "gaps" with a smile and, sometimes, with a song.

Thank you for listening.

…to friends

I am indebted to my friend, Rick Powell, President of Powell Incorporated, without whose confidence and encouragement this writing project would never have taken off. I hope he'll not be sorry.

And, without my wife of 53 years, my sweetheart, no way would it ever have been completed. She is my Board of Directors and Vice President of nit-picking, but her constructive criticism, and standby support, kept me on track.

A special thanks goes to Suki Kocheniak of Graphics, Mt. Kisco, New York, who understood what was going on in my head when I wasn't sure myself. Her smile and consistent patience is shown in every graphic line. Likewise, Gene Pharis of G and G Graphics in Atlanta, Georgia, made every digital dot of color an act of love. Plus, a warm hug and a kiss goes to Dr. Joanne Marien, Assistant School Superintendent for Instruction in Somers, New York, who listened to my fears and helped brush them away.

…and to his "little" helpers

Thanks to all who generously gave their time without counting minutes, including teachers and educational specialists in "Family and Consumer Sciences"; Dawn Brinson - Director, Furniture Discovery Center; Carl Vuncannon - Curator, Bernice Bienenstock Furniture Library; Dr. Richard Bennington; Bruce Miller; Andrew Cohen; Farooq Kathwari; Robin Campbell; Ruth Richards - Board of Cooperative Education Services, Westchester County, NY; Carolyn Allen Owsley, Willie Mae Williams, Susan C. McMillan, Annette Zylinski - Palm Beach, Dade and Broward County Public Schools; Ernie Friedman; Christianne Michaels; Julie Greiner; Allen Von Nopen; Fran Potvin; Joe Laneve; Clif Taylor; Richard Barentine; Doug L. Brackett; Bill DiPaolo; Dan Greer; Barry Wax; Russell Bienenstock; David Kaplan, Jr.; Charlie Green; Sarah and George Hundley; Brenda and Bob Stacy; Lester Craft; Rosanna Frank; Tony Bengel; Linda Horsik; all my children; Dr. William Bassett; Paul Hackett; Marjorie Walker; White G. Watkins; Mark A. Barford; Tom Inman; Liz Seymour; Fred Hutton; Ray Ringston; Tom Tilley; Paulette Rippley; David Perry; Wayne Wickstrom and all the "little" people in our industry who stand ten feet tall and are willing to help with a smile when a gray-haired grandpa pesters them.

Industry education partners who understand...

CORE SPONSORS

Century Furniture Industries
P.O. Box 608
Hickory, NC 28603

Heilig-Meyers*
12560 West Creek Parkway
Richmond, VA 23238

King Koil Sleep Products*
770 Transfer Road, Ste. 13
St. Paul, MN 55114

Leggett & Platt Incorporated
No. 1 Leggett Road
Carthage, MO 64836

Powell Incorporated
8631 Hayden Place, P.O. Box 1408
Culver City, CA 90232-1408

Stanley Furniture Company
P.O. Box 30
Stanleytown, VA 24168

Waverly Fabrics*
79 Madison Avenue
New York, NY 10016

SUPPORTERS

The Ashley Companies
1 Ashley Way
Arcadia, WI 54612

Beacon Hill*
One Design Center Place, Ste. 200
Boston, MA 02210-2309

Bloomingdale's*
919 Third Avenue
New York, NY 10022

Bush Industries
One Mason Drive
Jamestown, NY 14701

Centers of High Point*
126 North Park Street, P.O. Box 7366
Tupelo, MS 38802

First Factors Corporation
101 South Main Street, P.O. Box 2370
High Point, NC 27261

Furniture Today
7025 Albert Pick Road, Ste. 200
Greensboro, NC 27409

I.D. Kids
704 West Main Street
Teutopolis, IL 62467

Ladd Furniture Incorporated
4620 Grandover Parkway
Greensboro, NC 27417

Malden Mills
46 Stafford Street, P.O. Box 809
Lawrence, MA 01842

BOOSTERS

A. L. Myers Furniture
173 North Highland Avenue
P.O. Box 870, Rte. 9
Ossining, NY 10562

American Furniture Warehouse*
8501 Grant Street
Thornton, CO 80229

Box Props
P.O. Box 398
West Chicago, IL 60186-0398

Carl's Furniture Company*
6650 Federal Highway
Boca Raton, FL 33487

Classic Gallery Group
2009 Fulton Place
High Point, NC 27263

Compass Furniture
5025 Bloomfield Street
Jefferson, LA 70121

Dickerson Furniture Company
105 College Street
Booneville, MS 38829

Drexel Heritage Manhattan*
32 West 18th Street
New York, NY 10011

Dunk & Bright Furniture Co., Inc.
2648 South Salina Street
Syracuse, NY 13205

El Dorado Furniture*
4200 North West 167th Street
Miami, FL 33054

Ethan Allen Home Interiors-Canada*
6707 Elbow Drive South West
Calgary, Alberta, Canada T2V OE3

Ethan Allen Inc.*
Ethan Allen Drive
Danbury, CT 06813

Executive House
33 South 10th Street
Indiana, PA 15701

Julius M. Feinblum Real Estate, Inc.
175 Central Avenue South
Bethpage, NY 11714

Gabbert's
3501 Galleria
Edina, MN 55435

Garon's Ethan Allen Home Interiors*
8727 Loch Raven Boulevard
Towson, MD 21286-6276

Halpern's Ethan Allen Home Interiors
15053 South Dixie Highway
Miami, FL 33176

HFC - Home Furnishings Council
3411 Silverside Road
Rodney Building, Ste. 200
Wilmington, DE 19810

International Furniture Marketing
4720 Lincoln Boulevard, Ste 354
Marina Del Rey, CA 90292

IWFA - International Wholesale Furniture Association
164 South Main Street, Ste. 404
High Point, NC 27261

Johnny Janosik Furniture
RR 4, Box 1100
Laurel, MD 19956

Keller Manufacturing Co., Inc.
P.O. Box 8
Corydon, IN 47112

Klingman Furniture
P.O. Box 888
Grand Rapids, MI 49518-0888

Larmon Furniture Inc.
1324 East Seventh Avenue
Tampa, FL 33605

Lauman's Fine Furniture*
8650 Belair Road
Baltimore, MD 21236

La-Z-Boy Chair Company*
1284 North Telegraph Road
Monroe, MI 48162-3390

Legend Furniture
5555 North 51st Avenue, Ste. 106
Glendale, AZ 85301

Lifestyle Furnishings International
1300 National Highway
High Point, NC 27360

Market Square
305 West High Street
High Point, NC 27261

Maurice Villency*
200 Madison Avenue
New York, NY 10016

MGM Transport Corporation
70 Maltese Drive
Totowa, NJ 07512

National Furniture Mart
200 South Main Street
High Point, NC 27261

Noble Games
3333 East Broadway Avenue
Bismarck, ND 58501

Pacer Furniture Manufacturing, Inc.
2035 East 37th Street
Los Angeles, CA 90058

Richardson Brothers Company
P.O. Box 907 635CTH
Sheboygan Falls, WI 53085

Robb & Stucky*
P.O. Box 60479
Fort Myers, FL 33906

Rooms-To-Go*
11540 Highway 92 East
Seffner, FL 33584

Samsondale Furniture Galleries
36 Route 9W South
West Haverstraw, NY 10993

Samuel's Furniture Company*
2449 Scaper Cove
Memphis, TN 38114

San Francisco Mart
1355 Market Street, #294
San Francisco, CA 94103

Stacy's Ethan Allen Home Interiors*
1800 Banks Road
Margate, FL 33063

Tables and Chairs and More
1930 West Main Street
Stamford, CT 06902

THE Furniture Company
10116 Old Liberty Road
Liberty, NC 27298

Wickes Furniture*
351 Dundee Road
Wheeling, IL 60090

* Additional locations in other cities and states.

Table of Contents

		Page
Chapter 1	A learning experience can be fun.	1
Chapter 2	Homework for adults? Are you kidding? Nope.	4
Chapter 3	Twenty-four hours a day of Interior Environment Whose is it? The Space Planner's or the Client's?	9
Chapter 4	Who are you in color?	13
Chapter 5	"Stretch" a small room by thinking vertical.	19
Chapter 6	The secret space weapon. . . .closets.	24
Chapter 7	The Body-Measuring-Tape.	27
Chapter 8	Close your eyes and "see" your territory.	31
Chapter 9	Needs. Wants. Wishes. Sleep. Storage. Study.	30
Chapter 10	How to enjoy shopping for home furnishings. And make a salesperson your friend.	41
Chapter 11	The Couch Potato Fifty Percent Buying System. Cars, carpenters and tuna fish salad sandwich friends.	43
Chapter 12	Space planning with "Push-Together-Systems." Space planning with "Selective Eclectic" complements.	46
Chapter 13	Looking at furniture for the 1000th time and seeing it the first time with your eyes "open."	50
Chapter 14	Space Planner's Room Plan. Whose is it? It's really the client's.	56
Chapter 15	Grandpa Mike's Unbelievable Up-and-Down Bedroom Decorating System. Wow-e-e!	62

		Page
Chapter 16	This is the room size. This is what fits — how and why. This is what it costs. This is where we can buy it.	66
Chapter 17	Presentation before the Supreme Family Court.	72
Chapter 18	Grandpa Mike's Graduation Speech. Earning money can be fun too.	76
Chapter 19	• Pip's poem to her pen pal – "Jenni's Prayer"	78
	• Grandpa Mike's "What is it ?" Glossary Some things a Spatial Planner's client might ask…	79
	• "Little People" – Ten Feet Tall Make the World of Interior Environment spin…	80
	• Photo credits	82
Chapter 20	The World of Interior Environment — The Ideas, The Creations	83
	• Sleep needs seek their own levels	84
	• For storage and study needs in small spaces think vertical and push-together systems	86
	• Put two stars together and light a new eclectic one	88
	• Relax or sit up and take notice	90
	• Color, pattern, texture of textile design	92
Chapter 21	The World of Interior Environment	96
	• Some history Thomas Day, African American Craftsman	96
	• The language	98
	• The manufacturing highways	100
	• The consumer buyways	101
	• Heading for the manufacturing highways or the consumer buyways?	102

A Message Left For Carole Chalk on Her Kitchen Noteboard

Dear Mom:
My room has windows that I can see out
and walls that keep me safe and warm.
I can sleep. I can dress.
But there is no place to hide comfortably.

You care. I sure know that.
But, perhaps, I am selfish.
Because I dream a room of my very own,
not too big a room, but where through windows that are blinded
I can see far out into the universe.

I am not unhappy. I really love you a lot.
But Mom, Gee! I wish I had a bedroom that was all my own.

Can we please talk about it?
Thanks a million. Luv ya.

    Your daughter,

Pip!

Chapter 1

A learning experience can be fun.

Telephone rings

Carole Chalk:
    Hello, Grandpa Mike? Believe it or not, it's Carole Chalk.

Grandpa Mike:
    Carole? Is it really you?

Carole:
    It's not Mickey Mouse! How have you and Grandma Anita been? I don't really know why, but it seems that since you guys moved away from our block to the condo complex in Platte Village, you're like a million miles away, although it's only fifteen minutes by car. We miss seeing you.

Grandpa:
    We're fine, but still pooped out from the move. It's no fun moving from a large house to a two bedroom apartment. We sure miss all those closets.

Carole
    But not all those flights of steps.

Grandpa:
    You bet. Anyway, outside of our arthritis flare-ups, we're as young as seventy-six year olds with twenty year old minds can be.

Carole:
    Can't beat that.

Grandpa:
    We sure miss those kids of yours ringing our doorbell. And how are they doing these days?

Carole:
    They're great kids, Grandpa. Pip is really maturing beautifully and doing super in ninth grade. She's in three advanced classes. And Tommy is very busy with his computer program and graphics class. He's good at hockey, too. Can you imagine? He's almost twelve.

Grandpa:
    That's wonderful! We hear that you're taking up-date courses in nursing.

Carole:
    Right up to date. I also asked to be transferred from nights to the morning shift. Kids need more daytime attention, these days.

Grandpa:
Good for you. By coincidence, Carole, our grandchildren, just yesterday, asked how you and your gang were doing. They sure miss the great times we all spent together. And Grandma and I miss hearing your Pip and Tommy calling us "Grandma" and "Grandpa."

Are you calling for something special? Anything we can help with?

Carole:
Yes, there is, Grandpa. That's why I'm calling. Pip needs to have her bedroom refurnished. She brought it to my attention in a very cute way. She composed a poem and mounted it on my kitchen noteboard.

She's never complained, even though all her furniture pieces are hand-me-downs. And while I'm at it, I'd like to do Tommy's bedroom, too. He's younger but has a flair for design.

Are you still teaching the why's and wherefore's of spatial relationships and interior environment planning?

Grandpa:
Sure am. One class at the Putney Middle School and the other at Concordil Community College.

Carole:
Still in the ol' Grandpa Mike style that I sat through?

Grandpa:
Yep. Basic principles rarely change. But with computers and fresh machinery techniques there are always fresh angles. If you want me to help the kids redo their interior environments I'd be delighted. Do you think they can stand an old guy they call "Grandpa" as a teacher?

I love those kids but I'm still a demanding teacher and wouldn't want to lose their valuable friendships.

Carole:
Neither would they.

Grandpa:
And I still have that old styled idea that young people should earn what they receive, whether it's a room full of furnishings or an allowance. Especially these days when everything is expensive and money so hard to come by.

Carole:
I know the score, Grandpa. I, too, want it to be a learning experience but with loads of fun. And I know you can deliver both. In a few years, Pip will have to plan a dorm room or an apartment and your techniques will be a base she can build on.

Grandpa:
And I can't pass up a challenge. Please talk it over with the kids and I'll call you.

Carole:
Great! Please figure out your fee.

Grandpa:
> Fee? You've got to be kidding. You and those kids of yours are like part of our family. Eighteen years on the same block! We were there when they were born and later when they played with our grandchildren. Please don't insult me.

Carole:
> You win…and we win.

Grandpa:
> And while I remember, please ask Pip and Tommy to measure their rooms and put the measurements in sealed envelopes. I know those bedrooms are not that large but let's see if the three of us can figure out a way to "stretch" them. Take care, Carole. Grandma and I love you all. Ciao.

key terms

a. What is a "fee"?

b. What is a "condo complex"?

c. What does "ciao" mean? In what language?

d. What does CAD software stand for?

questions to explore

a. What do you think Pip means to say when she writes in her poem: "…there is no place to hide comfortably"?

b. and "…where through windows that are blinded I can see far out into the universe"?

c. Do you like the idea of her poem/letter? Why?

d. What does Grandpa Mike mean by "Let's see if the three of us can 'stretch' " the bedrooms which are not that large?

Chapter 2

Homework for adults? Are you kidding? Nope.

Door bell rings. Grandpa Mike answers and opens the door.

Grandpa:
    Pip! Tommy! Come on in. Let's see what you both look like.

Tommy:
    Grandpa Mike! How are you? Where's Grandma Anita?

Grandpa:
    She'll be here any moment. Had some last minute items on her shopping list so a kind neighbor took her to the supermarket. How was the bus ride?

Tommy:
    Not too bad. You know, Grandpa, you must be famous. When we asked the driver where your house number was he answered: "Oh! That's Grandpa Mike's place."

Pip:
    He's not famous, Tommy. He just knows everyone. When are you going to run for mayor, Grandpa?

Grandpa:
    When you're both old enough to vote for me.
    W-e-l-l, we're so happy that you both decided to visit with us and get started on your projects. Did you measure your rooms and seal the numbers in envelopes?

Tommy:
    Here's mine. Why are they sealed in envelopes?

Pip:
    Here's mine, too, Grandpa. Are they going to be opened on TV at the Academy Awards?

Grandpa:
    Well, well, Pip, I see, that outside of your height, you haven't changed much. And I'm glad. No, I'm not going to have Price, Waterhouse, the accounting firm, open them in Hollywood but we are going to open them once you guys learn how to measure a room without using a tape measure.

Tommy:
    Without a tape measure?

Grandpa:
    Right. You're going to use your body. Then we'll compare how close you got. But, for now, let's get started before Grandma shows up and insists you eat some special cookies. Let's hear what you wrote for your "dream room" assignment, Pip.

Pip:

> I hope this is what you want, sir: "I don't have to close my eyes to see it. I can even see it in the bright sunshine. There it is, floating in air like cotton candy caught up in the swoosh! of a ferris wheel. My own dream room set on a flying carpet of fluff. My own bedroom!"

Grandpa:

> I like the way you wrote that, Pip. I see why you're on the school paper. But isn't that more like daydreaming? It makes you feel good for a moment but in the long run, it's a time waster.

Pip:

> But, sir, that's how I see it. Is that wrong?

Grandpa:

> Absolutely not. It's really beautifully put, but to have a dream is another ball game. To have a dream is to take a step forward towards shaping a reasonable goal and goals, unlike daydreaming, can be transformed into the real thing.

Pip:

> How?

Grandpa:

> By doing your homework.

Tommy:

> Oh! No! Not more homework! Same old stuff. School and homework and homework and school.

Grandpa:

> Uh! Uh! School is not the only place requiring homework. Believe it or not, homework makes the world go round... yours and mine. Everyone does homework...everywhere. That's how things get done, for better or for worse... in proportion to how well the homework was done.
>
> Know anyone who is an on-the-road salesperson? Maybe a friend's parent or cousin? Ask one.

Pip:

> On-the-road?

Grandpa:

> Yes. That's a salesperson who travels from location to location selling products for a company she or he represents. They're called sales representatives, or sales reps for short. They do loads of homework...every night. If they don't do their homework (planning) the night before an important sales meetings with their customers, they miss the boat the following day. No homework, no planning, no products sold. They flunk the test.

Tommy:

> But, we're not selling anything, sir.

Grandpa:

Yes, you are. You're selling to yourself. I hear you're on the hockey team, Tommy. You practice regularly, right? That's homework. No practice, no win. And it doesn't matter whether it's a hockey team or an algebra club. Success and homework go hand in hand. If you'll just think about it, you'll find your own examples.

In the meantime, how about me getting some of my special hot chocolate ready for the cookies that Grandma is guaranteed to bring?
With whipped cream, of course.

Tommy:

I think I hear someone at the door. Must be Grandma Anita. I'll get it.

Grandma Anita comes in carrying groceries and stamping snow off her shoes.

Tommy:

Grandma Anita! Let me help you with those bundles.

Grandma:

Never mind the bundles, Tommy. Let's have a kiss or two. M-m-m, that warms me right up. Your turn, Pip, even high school young ladies still kiss a Grandma. Delicious! OK, into the kitchen. My guess is that Grandpa is in there making his special hot chocolate.

Tommy:

Gee! That was delicious, Grandma. What kind of cookies were they?

Grandma:

Homemade, by Mrs. Vorst, our neighbor, and she won't tell a soul what's in them. Years ago, she worked on them all night and now it's her secret weapon.

Tommy:

She sure did her homework.

Grandma:

Uh! Uh! kids. No washing dishes, this time. Go on back to the living room. I'll clean up because your Mom should be picking you up shortly.

Pip:

Y'know, I've been thinking, Grandpa. What you said about my room makes sense. But, then, what about my dream room?

Grandpa:
>Do you really want it or is it a passing fancy? Are you ready to try some practical, creative ideas? Because if you are, you can transform your dream room into a reality. It won't be flying in air but will stand— plunk! right in your room. A REAL dream room with real, dreamy things you can use.
>
>And as a bonus, while shaping that room and your thinking, you will discover simple techniques (tricks) that can truly make you an amateur, space planner. Not in space, but whammo! right in your own room.

Tommy:
>Me, too?

Grandpa:
>Both of you. And your first clients will be yourselves.

Pip:
>Clients? Ourselves?

Grandpa:
>Yes, Pip. A client is a customer who hires you do a job for her. An assignment.....

Tommy:
>Oh! Oh! Assignment!

Grandpa:
>As I was saying....You've been hired...selected...to do the job for yourself. You're the client and the planner. And if you do your homework you're going to have loads of fun. You'll learn where to start, how to calculate the cost of all the goodies you want and how to shop for them. And to make it all worthwhile, you will be prepared to sell your Mom on your dream room project.

Pip:
>Grandpa, honest, are you putting me on? First, I'm going to become an amateur space planner. Then, when I'm finished with the client, myself, I'm going to be able to pitch our Mom for the money.

Tommy:
>And am I included?

Grandpa:
>Yes, Tommy. Except that your homework is going to be a bit simpler, but not easier. One more point, Pip.

Pip:
>Oh! Oh!

Grandpa:
>During this interior environment adventure, you're liable to bump into the realization that you and your client are two different people. That one of you is just a carbon copy kid that hangs in with the rest of the girls at school, doing everything they do, while the other is an independent young lady that wants to be an original.
>
>A self-thinking person, who still holds on to her valuable friendships.

Pip:
You're sure you're not putting me on, Grandpa?

Grandpa:
Never. I guarantee it. Not only that, you'll recognize the difference between a chest of drawers, a lingerie chest and an armoire.

Pip:
What did you call those last two?

Grandpa:
A lingerie chest and an armoire.

Pip:
That did it, Grandpa. Sign me on as your client.

Tommy:
I'm not sure I understand all of this client stuff, Grandpa. But if Grandma Anita can find out how her neighbor makes those secret cookies, so I can tell my Mom, that will be my dream.

Anyway, I'm sure I can convince Mom that I know what I'm doing when I draw it all out on my computer with Computer Assisted Design software. Count me in, sir.

Grandpa:
Tommy, have you ever dreamed about being President of the United States?

lingerie chest

armoire

key terms

a. What is "accounting"?

b. What is an "accounting firm"?

questions to explore

a. Give two examples of persons who do homework and don't go to school.

b. What kind of homework?

c. List two rooms in your home where someone planned the space.

Chapter 3

*Twenty-four hours a day of Interior Environment.
Whose is it? The Space Planner's or the Client's?*

Pip:
    Grandpa, I was thinking about my dream room again. And I'd like to be a bit more realistic this time. So can I try again?

Tommy:
    Can't wait.

Grandpa:
    Easy, Tommy. Any week now you'll be trying.

Tommy:
    With poetry stuff?

Grandpa:
    Who knows? We'll see. Go on, Pip, I really want to hear what you wrote.

Pip:
    Thank you, Grandpa.
    "Music fills my room. It doesn't come pouring out of the side walls but rather as if the speakers were planted in the floor. I can feel the notes rumbling underfoot like an oil well that is aching to erupt. But they don't. Slowly they climb up the walls and gently, very gently, bump across the ceiling and rain, ever so lightly, down the other walls, into my mind. I relax because it's a song I know the words to. Mom plays it on the piano."

Grandpa:
    Pip, that's beautiful. And it sounds to me you'd like to allot space for music and music equipment in your room. Is that right?

Pip:
    Absolutely. But does it sound silly the way I put it?

Grandpa:
    Not to me. Sometimes when I hear beautiful music I even get the chills. Good for you, Pip.

Tommy:
    When do I get my turn?

Pip:
    When I go to sleep.

Grandpa:
    Anytime you're ready, Tommy. Well, let's move on. To start out, remember, you are the room planner. The interior environment planner.

Tommy:
>Interior environment? What's that, Grandpa?

Grandpa:
>Almost everything you touch...and everywhere you go. Unlike outdoor environment, interior environment surrounds you all day long. It is planned, designed and created by someone in the home furnishings industry and it is everywhere you go.

Pip:
>Everywhere we go? How about school?

Grandpa:
>That's an easy one. The desks, the chairs, the blackboards, the flooring, the windows, the ceiling and the clothing hooks, to name just a few. Now you guys try it. How about a restaurant?

Tommy:
>Like a McDonald's?

Grandpa:
>I wasn't thinking of that one but why not try it.

Tommy:
>The chairs, the tables, the place where you order, the ovens, the refrigerators, the wallpaper and all the dishes and utensils. Gee! I am learning!

Grandpa:
>More than learning you're thinking, Tommy. How about a hospital?

Pip:
>No question. A movie theater?

Tommy:
>Easy. An office?

Pip:
>Or a car?

Tommy:
>A car?

Pip:
>Of course. There are cushioned seats and carpeting plus the dashboard, doors and ceiling are, usually, upholstered in fabrics. Right?

Grandpa:
>One hundred percent right, Pip. So before we meet, next week, keep looking around and make a simple list of all these interior environment surroundings and what's in them. I call them home and specialty furnishings.
>   And they all have to be thought out by room planners like you're going to be. No matter where you turn you'll find an area and furnishings that someone planned and had created.

Pip:
>That's exciting, Grandpa. Can't wait to get started on my interior environment. I mean my client's interior environment.

Grandpa:
>You're on the right track, guys. Remember, you're the client and the planner. Now, in order to do a meaningful job, you've got to get the planner, you, out of your client's way. Which, of course, is your way.

Tommy:
>Wait a minute. I've got it! It's like Abbott and Costello and the "Who's on first?" thing. Right, Grandpa?

Pip:
>Wait a minute. W-a-i-t a m-i-n-u-t-e!! Let me see if I understand what I got myself into here. First, I'm the room planner. Second, I'm also the client. Third, therefore, my room is now my client's room. A-n-d, if I get out of my own way, I'll be able to do a better planning job for my client...who is me. Right?

Grandpa:
>Right on. You see, Pip, choices will have to be made and you must not impose your planning personality on that of your client's. Because if you do then it will become the room you want and not the one your client needs. Any questions?

Tommy:
>Yes. Does Grandma still have any of those neighbor's cookies around?

Pip:
>It's a bit too much for me, Grandpa. Try again.

Grandpa:
>Gladly, Pip. What it all boils down to is simply this. Your client will have a lot of decisions to make in getting her room planned. You have to help her. And the best way for you to help her is for you to first understand who you are in interior environment.
>
>You have to analyze, which means examine, what you seem to like and dislike in things that surround you. And, if possible, to know if and why you might want to change them. Got it?

Pip:
>Not all of it, sir. But I'm trying.

Grandpa:
>You, as the planner, can't go off daydreaming. You have to be practical so that your client can end up with realistic choices and a reasonable budget. The name of this game is to get your hardworking Mom to redo your client's room. How? By presenting a functioning, imaginative room plan that will fit a fair money budget. If you don't, you, as the planner, will have failed the assignment and your client will be out of luck.

Pip:
>In other words, I've got to know what I'm doing and be practical about it.

Grandpa:
>You said it in a lot less words than I did, Pip. Bravo! for you. A good planner knows herself and like a good psychologist doesn't confuse her client with impossible choices. Did I put it on too thick, Pip? Are you still with me?

Pip:
>I'm with you, Grandpa. Get me out of my way.

Tommy:
And some cookies for me, too, please.

Pip:
And, this time, I think I need a couple for myself, too, Grandpa. How do I get started?

Grandpa:
With these cookies and a glass of chocolate milk. Then go out and buy yourself the book *The Joy of Self Analysis*.

Pip:
In what bookstore? And who is the author?

Grandpa:
In no bookstore and you'll be the author. Go down to the supermarket and buy yourself a hardcover, ruled notebook. Take Tommy along, please, and get one for him, too, in another color.
   Wait! Do you two like lemon cake? Great! I'll have one ready at our next session.

Pip and Tommy:
With cherry chip, fat free, yogurt, Grandpa?

Grandpa:
Cherry chip on lemon cake? Hm-m-m… I never thought of that color combination. Pink, red and white on a yellow background. It's always been vanilla for me. Must be a cake decorating habit with me. Cherry chip? Very interesting. I'll have to analyze that.

key terms

a. What is a "client"?

b. What is "interior environment" air quality?

questions to explore

a. List three professionals that have "clients."

b. List three areas of interior environment that Tommy and Pip did not think of.

c. Do you think that interior environment air quality is as important as outdoor environment air quality? Does it matter where more time is spent?

d. Which aspect of interior environment air quality?

Chapter 4

Who are you in color?

Doorbell rings. Grandpa yells from the kitchen:

Grandpa:
> I'll be right there, kids.

Pip and Tommy:
> Hi, Grandpa. We're here.

Grandpa:
> Good. How's Mom? Tired, I'll bet.

Pip:
> You bet, Grandpa. Especially with those new classes she's taking.

Grandpa:
> Would you, please, ask her to give me a ring when she can so that we can arrange to meet at your house next week? She can call as late as eleven because I'm working on my new illustrated book. Did you buy the hardcover notebooks?

Tommy:
> We sure did. This one is mine.

Grandpa:
> Careful. Don't get cherry chip on it.

Tommy:
> Wow!

Pip:
> I'm tired. We had a double Phys Ed period this afternoon. But I'm ready.

Grandpa:
> Thanks. I'll make it short, today. On the first page of the notebook, somewhere down the middle, print in capital letters, "The Joy of Self Analysis." Then on the line below it, sign your full name and don't forget your middle initial. It's impressive for an author and room planner.

Pip:
> Middle initial? I don't even have a middle name!

Tommy:
> Neither do I.

Grandpa:
> You really are deprived kids. Well, then, let's adopt one. Choose one you've always wanted.

Pip:
>How about Jennifer? I always liked that one. Pip J.Chalk. Sounds good.

Grandpa:
>Rings the bell with me. But spell it Jenni and you've got it made because when you become famous as a poet or author the reporters will ask 'Why Jenni?' and you'll have all kinds of charming answers. Alright, now sign it. Beautiful!
> How about you, Tommy?

Tommy:
>I like Brandon.

Pip:
>Brandon?

Tommy:
>Yes, that was my teacher's name in third grade. I liked him.

Pip:
>Tommy B. Chalk. I think that sounds important. Like a President of the United States.

Grandpa:
>Congratulations, kids. You now own the first author's signed copy of this year's best seller: *The Joy of Self Analysis* by you!

Pip:
>*The Joy of Self Analysis?* By me? What do I know about self analysis?

Grandpa:
>Nothing.

Pip:
>Do you know anything about self analysis, Grandpa?

Grandpa:
>Nothing.

Pip:
>Nothing? W-e-l-l, that adds up to a double nothing...zilch. So what's this all about? Wait! Please don't answer. I promised to go along with this adventure so I'll wait and listen for a while.

Grandpa:
>Thanks for the vote of confidence, Pip. OK, now here goes the self analysis. Stretch out over there and relax.

Pip:
>How's this for relaxation?"

Grandpa:
>No, not on the floor. Right there on the sofa. No, not that one. That one is a love seat. It's shorter and seats only two. A sofa seats three. Tommy you take the big, leather arm chair. Everyone relax.

Tommy:

Gee! I feel like I'm a guest on one of those TV shows that ask you all kinds of questions.

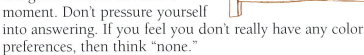

Grandpa:

OK you two. Relax, but don't fall asleep. Now just ask yourselves: "Do any particular colors make me feel good?" Think about it a moment. Don't pressure yourself into answering. If you feel you don't really have any color preferences, then think "none."

Tommy:

I'm thinking.

Pip:

My mind's a blank.

Grandpa:

If, on the other hand, you do have some color preferences, list them on the next page of your masterpiece.
   Hold it! Hold it! Forget it. I'm wrong.

Pip:

You wrong? I don't believe it. Not you, Grandpa?

Grandpa:

Yes, me. Let's start all over. Don't list your color preferences. Instead list the colors you don't like. Kids are always saying, "I love sky blue," or "I adore hot pink." In effect, they are prejudiced against other colors of the rainbow and shy away from using them in clothing or even posters. They just don't feel comfortable with them. They're too loud or too feminine or too masculine or just zilch. They're afraid to try them.

Pip:

That's interesting.

Grandpa:

So again, instead of thinking about colors you enjoy, think about colors you are prejudiced against and why? Many times it's not a color that turns you off, but rather it's an association with something else: Like a person, a memorable event or a place. All unpleasant.

Pip:

You know, Grandpa, you may have something there. I remember Ms. Korston, my teacher in fifth grade. She always wore an orange and white polka dot scarf. I never liked that scarf, especially on surprise test days. I never really liked Ms. Korston, either. Gee! I wonder which feeling came first, disliking the scarf or disliking Ms. Korston?

Tommy:

I don't like purple. It makes me feel sad when I see it flying at the church or at the firehouse.

Grandpa:
>Now you two are thinking and I'm proud of you. You're relaxing without a TV being on and it's stimulating your mind. So please sit up, turn to page two and list a few of your N.G. colors...and accompanying thoughts, too, if you'd like.
>Take your time and get some fun out of this. You'll be surprised where it leads to.

Pip:
>Y'know, I might like this analysis stuff. It's fun asking yourself questions and having no one around to hear if the answers are wrong.

Tommy:
>How about us doing a color wheel?

Grandpa:
>We're not going to do a color wheel, today. You're eleven years old and should know that red, blue and yellow are the primary colors. 'Primary' meaning that they are pure colors, number one, basic, on which all the other colors are built.

Tommy:
>I know that.

Grandpa:
>Good, And we're not going to talk about the secondary, number two (1 plus 1) colors, either. You should know by now that they're arrived at by mixing two of the primary colors, in equal amounts. Red and blue make...

Pip and Tommy:
>Violet.

Grandpa:
>Good. How do you get orange?

Pip and Tommy:
>Red and yellow.

Tommy:
>And blue and yellow mix up as green.

Grandpa:
>It's the tertiary, number three colors (1 plus 1 plus 1) that I'd like us to discuss. The ones that are mixed by taking a secondary color a (1 plus 1) and adding more of one of the primary colors already in it.

Tommy:
>Try us.

Grandpa:
>All right, I will. If you take a secondary green (1 plus 1) and add an extra snip of primary yellow to it, what (1 plus 1 plus 1 tertiary) color will pop up?

Pip:
>Tertiary yellow-green.

Tommy:
>The next one's mine.

Grandpa:
> Likewise, add more primary blue to the secondary green and.....?

Tommy:
> Tertiary blue-green. Gee! It feels like being on "Jeopardy!"

Grandpa:
> Very good. And it goes right down the line: Violet can become tertiary blue-violet or red-violet and orange can become red-orange or yellow-orange. For the benefit of professional artists, designers and printers who live with color all day long, there are code numbers for colors to make them more accurate when required in printing on fabrics or in books.

Pip:
> Grandpa, I think I also once heard different names for tertiary colors like plum, mulberry, russet and flame.

Grandpa:
> That's super, Pip, and correct, too. In fact, if you want to really see how many different shades and names there are then stop in at a good paint store, tell the manager about this adventure and politely–I repeat–politely ask for a collection of paint chips.

Tommy:
> Paint chips?

Pip:
> Yes, Tommy. They are little paper strips of color to help people needing paint to take home and study before they buy the real thing. They hold them up to colors, like in fabric they already own, to see if it is pleasing to them.

Grandpa:
> When you get the chips, see if you can figure out which primary color was added to the secondary (1 plus 1) mix to get the tertiary of the strip. It's fun.
> And that's that for color. All I wanted to do is have you know how to recognize colors you want to use and how they are constructed.

Pip:
> That's all? Aren't we going to talk about colors that don't go together and all that stuff?

Grandpa:
> Nope. Because there is no such "stuff." Color is a personal matter. It's like music. One fan's Heavy Metal is another's Mozart symphony. It's a matter of education by walking around with your eyes "open". "Open" meaning to appreciate.

Tommy:
> Open?

Grandpa:
> "Open" meaning to be sensitive to color in nature, a painting, a dress fabric or furniture fabric coverings, to say the least. Little by little, you will adopt, reject or modify your own color relationships.

Tommy:
> Doesn't that make me a copycat?

Grandpa:
> It sure does but the painting you're "copying" was never an original in color, either. It's an adaptation like yours will be. Only you're going to put a new spin on it because there really aren't any new color combinations, just new applications.

Pip:
> I think I once heard that. Who said it?

Grandpa:
> I just did.

Pip:
> Oh!

Grandpa:
> Sorry, I was carried away for the moment. Let's get back to your notebooks. Next week I will try to have a color wheel for you to paste in your book. It's no more than a circle of color chips. When you have the time, you'll study the names of the colors and take note of where they set on the wheel. It'll be interesting because the arrangement starts with the primary colors and you both are experts on red, blue and yellow. Right?

Tommy:
> Grandpa, I really like this color project. I wish I could learn more about it for my computer science course.

Grandpa:
> That's wonderful, Tommy, because there's a whole world of color to learn about: from the range of rainbow colors to scientist Isaac Newton's prism experiment; from the rods and cones message center on the retina of your eye to the design of the infinitesimal dots on an electronic chip for video. We'll talk about the miracle of light and color.
>
> I love you kids and it's a privilege spending time with you. Take care and keep those eyes "open"....wide open.

key terms

a. What is a "retina"? What is its function?

b. What is a "prism"?

questions to explore

a. What is Isaac Newton's prism experiment?

b. Name 3 colors that say something to us.

c. Name 3 colors that you never wear. Why?

Chapter 5

"Stretch" a small room by thinking vertical.

Door bell rings at Carole Chalk's apartment.

Tommy:
I'll get it, Mom. It's got to be Grandpa Mike.

Tommy opens the door.

Grandpa:
Is anyone home?

Tommy:
Only us chickens, Grandpa. Come on in and let me have your coat. Boy! It must be cold out there.

Grandpa:
Sure is, Tommy. Where's Mom and Pip?

Tommy:
Mom is finishing up in the kitchen and Pip is hiding in her room.

Grandpa:
Hiding? Who from?

Tommy:
You, sir. She's been straightening it out for three days. I wonder how long it will take me when it's my turn.

Grandpa:
Well, you'd better get started tomorrow. Next week is your D-Day. Good luck.

Carole:
Grandpa! Good to see you. Please excuse the uniform. I got stuck at the hospital and haven't had a chance to slip into something unbusiness-like. Wow! What a day! That ice out there sure kept us busy. How about a cup of tea to warm your bones.
   Pip! Grandpa is here. She's been in isolation all afternoon. Thank goodness she had a half day off for teachers' conference.

Pip:
Hi, Grandpa. I think it's ready.

Grandpa:
It's?

Pip:
Yes, my room. I really tried hard to make it presentable, sir. I hope it will be OK with you.

Grandpa:
> I've seen them all, Pip, and I've one of my own, too. So don't you worry a bit. Many's the day I wouldn't have a visitor in my home office, especially after Grandma chews me out for sorting reports on my floor. But, without her regular inspections I'd never straighten out. Relax and let's get started.

Tommy:
> I'm disappearing, sir. I'll say good night after I finish my homework. I've got to make a verbal report tomorrow. Scary!

Pip:
> Here's the patient, Grandpa.

Carole:
> Looks pretty good, Pip. Maybe Grandpa would show up here regularly.

Grandpa:
> Gee! gang, I'm a teacher and a friend. Not a health inspector.

Carole:
> I'll put the teapot up and make myself look normal. See ya in a bit.

Pip:
> You know, Grandpa, I've been thinking. It's amazing how you get away with not calling all this stuff homework. Instead you just say: "Think about this" or "Take a look at that." Pretty sharp, sir. I'm going to remember that when I'm a teacher. But, I still love you.

Grandpa:
> Thank you, Pip. I'll have to make a note of that observation for my I'll-write-a-book-some-day file. Now tell me, how long did you take to look over this interior environment of your client's?

Pip:
> Well, you have to remember, I know my client a long, long time.

Grandpa:
> You sure do. But how long did you spend looking it over?

Pip:
> A long time, About five or six minutes.

Grandpa:
> Five or six minutes? That's no long time. That's just a glimpse. And a glimpse is like viewing things from a car going 55 miles an hour, while a thorough look is like an examination under a microscope for about half an hour.
>
> Let's try it together. Please stand in the middle of the room, close one eye, form a telescope with your hands and imagine yourself squinting through a video camera viewer as you slowly arc around the room. Nice and easy. Great!
>
> Now try it once more and a lot, lot slower. Run your camera up and down each of the four walls.

Pip:

Very interesting! It's like viewing a stranger's room. Like seeing it for the first time. Gee! I should have had film in the camera so I could enter it for a prize on one of those "Funny Video" shows.

Grandpa:

Well, you're going to have a record of it, anyway, because the next step is to take a wall and floor inventory of your client's room...wall by wall.

Pip:

An inventory, sir?

Grandpa:

Yes, Pip, that's a listing of what someone owns. That's why when you select something at a store in a mall they have to check their inventory. And if it's not "in inventory" they tell you that they're "out of stock."

OK, let's set up an inventory on a separate page and divide it in thirds. Then start listing all the items you saw on the video sweep starting from the wall with the door on it. Write slowly, clearly and skip two lines between each item.

Pip:

Two lines between each item? Grandpa! I learned that in second grade.

Grandpa:

Well then, Pip, you were two years late. According to one famous author you should have learned that in kindergarten. So, you see, second grade is really an advanced class. However, if you stick to this guide, it will give you ample space for corrections or additions. And when you finish the inventory, you'll be able to read it back, too. All this may sound like little kid stuff, but clear record keeping forms the base for good performance.

So enter everything that is stuck to a wall: Posters, signs, photos, mirror, hanging lamps and drawings. Don't rush. Do it systematically...one wall at a time.

Pip:

Why are we doing all this, Grandpa?

Grandpa:

That's a good question, Pip. I was hoping you'd ask. One, is to make you realize how much clutter there is on these walls. Two, is to make you aware that all bedrooms – large and small – have the same height, generally, eight feet. Three, is to help you see that vertical space is precious and has to be utilized for storage when horizontal space is inadequate in small bedrooms.

That's how planners "stretch" rooms. By utilizing wall space. And you can't "stretch" them by climbing up the walls with storage drawers or cabinets or shelves when all this paraphernalia is stuck to those walls. Paraphernalia, you have to see to enjoy.

Pip:

H-m-m-m. That makes sense.

Grandpa:

Good. And while you're at it, Pip, note what you're standing on.

Pip:

Standing on, Grandpa? It's the floor, isn't it?

Grandpa:
>It sure is. But what is partially covering that floor?

Pip:
>Carpeting. Right?

Grandpa:
>Not exactly. Carpeting extends wall-to-wall and is tacked down around the borders with hidden wooden strips that are nailed to the floor under it. Does your carpet do that?

Pip:
>Nope. It doesn't stretch to the walls. In fact, I notice, it seems to slide around a bit.

Grandpa:
>It does, because it is not carpeting but rather an area rug that can be lifted for cleaning or moved to different positions. It is framed by the bare wood flooring under it. Bedroom area rugs are usually comparatively inexpensive, generally washable and woven in the United States on intricate, large machines. More costly ones, for living rooms or dining rooms, are imported from countries in the Middle East and Turkey or India where most are woven by women in villages, by hand. The exquisite, intricate patterns that they weave have been handed down from mother to daughter for centuries.

Pip:
>Amazing! I've walked on that area rug a million times and never bothered to look once at what I was walking on.

Grandpa:
>And that's exactly what this exercise is all about, Pip. To make you aware of everything that surrounds you in interior environment. To make you curious, to ask questions and to search for answers.
> Finally, include in your inventory, everything that is not a piece of furniture.

Pip:
>Like my stuffed animals?

Grandpa:
>Yes, all of them, plus the dolls, the guitar, the hi-fi speakers and the astronomy telescope that you saw the Bopp-Hale Comet with. Your aquarium is not furniture, either.

Pip:
>Please don't ask me to list the fish, too. Grandpa, does that client of mine ever throw anything out?

Grandpa:
>I'm afraid not. That's why this room seems so crowded, although there's only a twin bed, a night table, a single dresser and a small, inadequate writing desk in it. It's a common problem.

Carole shows up at the open door.

Carole:
>Here's your cup of tea, Grandpa, and one for you too, Pip. How are you doing, honey?

Pip:
> I can't believe what I'm seeing, Mom. Now I know what Grandpa Mike meant by keeping our eyes open.

Grandpa:
> Thanks a million, Carole. No, Pip, you don't have to inventory the fish in the aquarium....but if you wish to list their colors, for posterity, it might be exciting.
>
> Where's Tommy, Carole?

Carole:
> He's out cold. That speech assignment did him in. Anything you want me to tell him, Grandpa?

Grandpa:
> Yes, please. Tell him I'll see him in two days and that Pip will fill him in on what we touched on today. We'll start on Wednesday with his closet inventory.

Pip:
> Closet inventory! Wow! Am I glad that we didn't start there in my room!

Grandpa:
> The reason we didn't was that I knew, from experience, that the closet was holding all the things you had gathered up from the floor and I was afraid it would all come crashing down on us when you opened the door. Seriously, you're doing just fine, Pip. Thanks again for the tea, Carole. Ciao.

computer desk with hutch

key terms

a. What is "D-Day"?

questions to explore

a. What do banks inventory for their clients?

b. How do clients know what their personal inventory amounts to?

c. What countries weave area rugs by hand?

Chapter 6

The secret space weapon…closets.

Grandpa visits with Tommy

Grandpa:
Did Pip explain the wall and floor inventory session that we had?

Tommy:
Yes, she did, Grandpa and here is mine. Notice the difference?

Grandpa:
Sure do. No teddy bears or dolls but your share of hockey sticks, posters, a microscope, a giant Cal Ripken figure and what's this? Cribbage boards? You play cribbage, Tommy?

Tommy:
Yes, I do. I love it. Mom and I play whenever we can. As you see I have a few boards. Even one that folds for travelling.

Grandpa:
I can't believe it! Do you know that Grandma and I are cribbage buffs? We play cribbage almost every night before we go to sleep. We were taught the game by a buddy of mine during World War II. Gee! That's over 50 years ago!

And would you believe? We once had a cocktail table…that's a low table about 14″ high that stands in front of a sofa…that was hewn from a large tree trunk and made into a jumbo, 30″ long cribbage board complete with handmade pegs. Imagine! A cocktail table-cribbage board!

Tommy:
A 30″ cribbage board! All of mine are little ones about a foot long that sit on the kitchen table. Do you have any other special boards and pegs?

Grandpa:
We sure do. I'll have Grandma show them to you when you visit. We have a fine mahogany veneer one with ivory inlays and ivory pegs, one with tin trim and a tiny wooden one about 5 inches long. And talking about games, we have a marble checkerboard with a fine set of carved wood, chess pieces. Years ago these games were made by furniture artisans who not only made furniture with hand tools but knew all about the special qualities and properties of different woods.

Tommy:
I think it's fun collecting such stuff.

Grandpa:
> They are not stuff, Tommy. They are works of art just like a fine piece of sculpture. And by coincidence, just a few months ago, at an international exhibit, I bumped into a cribbage board of hand selected hardwoods that had a pegging surface of full grain lambskin leather. Unbelievable! modern craftsmanship!
>
> You know, it might be fun looking up the origin and history of cribbage and boards. I think it all started in England a long time ago, because the "Jack" card is called "His Nibs." And that's an English colloquialism.

Tommy:
> Colloquialism?

Grandpa:
> Yes, that's an expression or word used in a given region or local area. There are many such words used in locales of our country, too. A hero sandwich in New York might be a sub in New England.
>
> Well, let's get on with that closet of yours before I forget what I came here for. Ready or not, open up.

Tommy:
> Remember, Grandpa, you asked for it!

Grandpa:
> Stand back, Tommy, it might explode! Hey! It didn't! It's crowded but neat.

Tommy:
> Why did you want me to inventory my walls, floor and closet, Grandpa?

Grandpa:
> Because, as I explained to Pip, children's bedrooms are generally small and therefore when you furnish them you have to think "vertical" up the walls instead of just horizontal, around the walls. Remember, no matter how small a room is, it's always 8 feet high and that's why the walls have to be kept clear of things that are stuck or nailed to them. They get in the way of stacked furniture.

Tommy:
> But, Grandpa, I love those posters.

Grandpa:
> And I love my paintings but they have to be positioned after the fundamental needs of the client have been satisfied. A closet on the other hand, is a secret space weapon. If it weren't behind a door it would add about five more running feet to this room.

Tommy:
> A secret space weapon? Sounds like "Star Wars."

Grandpa:
> It's Star Wars when it's organized, but it's Jurassic Park when it's all cluttered. The trick is to recognize what you use a closet for.

Tommy:
> For hanging clothes, right?

Grandpa:
> Of course. Bulky items like jackets and pants and lighter things that wrinkle easily, like shirts. Items that if stored in drawers take up too much space. Now, Tommy, sort of walk into that closet and see how high it is and how many shelves and rods there are built into it.

Tommy:
> There's one pole and one shelf in it. And the height of the closet is the same as the ceiling of the room and you said that was 8 feet.

Grandpa:
> That's good figuring, Tommy, and that's your secret space weapon. Your client is only using half his closet. All the space underneath the top row is wasted because it is not organized. You can put another rod in it for more trousers, or shelves for heavy sweaters and then line up shoes and sneakers on the floor. That's thinking vertical.

Tommy:
> Gee! Grandpa! That means my client can take a lot of the things from the drawers in the furniture and hang them up in the closet. No wonder those drawers are always getting jammed up.

Grandpa:
> One young client I once worked with had a drawer full of heavy lead toy soldiers and so the bottom collapsed. Drawers are not made for that kind of abuse. When we were finished planning, underwear ended up in the drawer and the soldiers were lined up in a small cabinet with glass doors that he found in a junk shop.

Tommy:
> You know what, I'm going to ask Mr. George, my computer teacher, if I can diagram my closet on the CAD screen. I'll bet he'll say "Yes."

Grandpa:
> I'm sure he will. And when you're finished show it to Pip and tell her about your secret space weapon. She has a double door closet in her room. It's about one-and-a-half times the size of yours. You were really on the thinking-ball today, Tommy.
>
> By the way, Tommy, what do you like the most about playing cribbage?

Tommy:
> The challenge of trying to do the most with the hand I'm dealt.

Grandpa:
> You know, Tommy, that's exactly what Grandma said when I once asked her that question.

Tommy:
> I like two more things, Grandpa. One, to play cribbage you have to learn to add quickly and to peg fast. So, I'm lucky I'm good in math. But the best thing about cribbage playing is that it's not mean like many other games. It's fun, even if you lose. We never get upset.
>
> Thanks for coming, sir. Ciao.

Chapter 7

The Body-Measuring-Tape.

One late afternoon, a week later in the Chalk apartment. Grandma and Grandpa are busy in Carole's kitchen.

Pip: *(Calling from her bedroom)*
Grandma! I hope you're making your special mushroom and barley soup that's thick enough to cut with a knife.

Grandma:
I'm not telling, but it surely isn't something out of a can. In the meantime, keep your mind on your homework so we'll all be ready to eat when Mom comes home. I understand that's a rarity in this house what with Mom's on-again-off-again schedule at the hospital.

Grandpa:
How does this chocolate icing look, Ma? Is it smooth enough?

Grandma:
Couldn't be better if I did it myself. Do you think Carole will mind us surprising her? Remember, she puts in a hard day's work.

Grandpa:
She'll love it. If nothing else, at least, we'll finally be reciprocating for the great evening she put together for your seventy-fifth birthday.

Grandma:
That's hard to beat. And remember, you want to start on Pip's room tonight, so don't start telling one of your long dinner stories.

Grandpa:
Gee! It's great to still be appreciated after fifty-three years of marriage.

Grandma:
You bet. And to the same woman, too.

Carole:
What a meal! What unexpected company! And what a beautiful evening! With this kind of tender loving care I'll never mind birthdays and growing older, anymore.

Grandma:
Don't ever mind growing older, Carole. That's the best gift anyone can receive, particularly when it's delivered with so much love from your children. They're beautiful.

Carole:
> I know, Grandma. And the two of you are the finishing touch. I'm sure glad that Pip wrote me that poem-message and brought us all so close together, again.

Grandma:
> Let's you and I clean up so that Grandpa can get started with the children's room plans. We'll have dessert after the lesson and that will make Grandpa speed things up a bit. He never can wait too long for dessert.

Grandpa:
> Yep. Let's all do a blitz cleanup and come right back here to the dining room table. That way we won't have to travel too far for the dessert.

Grandma:
> I told you, Carole. It's amazing! how the promise of dessert can do miracles. The dishes have already been blitz washed clean.

Grandpa:
> The lesson for today is "The Body Measuring Tape" and here are your startup kits. One for each of you: A tape measure. A pad and a pencil. Carole, you, Tommy and Pip are one team. Grandma and I, the other.
>
> Now everyone span their right hand on the table as if you were going to play a piano cord. Measure it from tip to tip. It should range from seven to nine inches.

Pip:
> Gosh! Mom's span is ten inches.

Carole:
> Tommy's is seven.

Grandpa:
> So is Grandma's.

Tommy:
> Pip's is ten, too.

Grandma:
> Grandpa's is nine.

Grandpa:
> Enter your own span size on your pad. Now everyone, please stand alongside the dining room table. Measure the height of your team members' waistlines. I said the height. It probably will average about thirty nine inches.

Carole:
> Right on the button.

Grandma:
> Same average for our team.

Grandpa:
> Please enter your own figure on your pad. Figure? That's funny. Now, how would you guess the approximate height of the dining room table?

Pip:
> Well, we see that it's less than the height of our waistline.

Grandma:
> Right.

Tommy:
> And we know that our hand span averages about eight inches.

Carole:
> So all we have to do is span from our waist down to the table top.

Everyone:
> And that leaves about thirty inches.

Grandpa:
> And that is correct. Now some measuring oldies: Enter the measurement of your shoed foot. Then have a team member measure your height against a wall. Be careful that you all measure from the top of the head and not the hairdo.

Pip:
> What's left, Grandpa?

Grandpa:
> Your body and arms. Stand as close as you can facing a wall and stretch out one arm. Measure across the back plus one arm right up to the finger tips. It's amazing how many will be almost exactly the height to the waistline. Good. Now add the other arm. The overall length should approach six feet.
> And how many inches is that?

Everyone:
> Seventy-two inches.

Grandpa:
> And the winner is: "Everyone!" Now sit down and I'll bring in the dessert prizes.

Carole:
> Delicious! Delicious! Who made this cake and frosting?

Grandpa:
> I did...with a bit of help from Sara Lee. But the layer of strawberries and rhubarb in the middle is all mine.

Grandma:
> Gee! It's awfully quiet around this table. Who will be the first one to ask THE obvious question?

Pip:
> I'll volunteer. Grandpa, why do we need all these body tape measurements when all we need is a real tape?

Grandpa:
> I just knew that with my darling sweetheart being here that question would come up very quickly. And here is my answer. I said my answer.
>
> We all know from experience that the tape I distributed will not be glued to you every moment of the day. In addition, when you will see an interesting piece of furniture in a neighbor's home, or a museum, you certainly can't pull out a tape to measure it. That's an impolite no, no.
>
> But you will always have your "Body Tape Measure" with you. Some day when you'll be led through a college dorm or an apartment or an office you'll be thrilled you stored it in your mind and eye. Right?

Everyone:
> It's possible.

Grandpa:
> And years from today you'll want to impress a salesperson trying to sell you kitchen appliances. You'll want to let him know that you know the score. And you will say, accurately: "That refrigerator is a span too wide. It just won't fit between my kitchen counter and wall."

Everyone:
> Wow-e-e!

Grandpa:
> Thank you, ladies and gentleman. What I've attempted here is to start you to "see" measurements with your eye and to "feel" spatial relationships. They won't be exact but they won't be way, way off, either. Experienced designers, layout planners and architects do it all the time. That's how they, initially, "size up" a room. You will, too.

Grandma:
> That was a long speech, Grandpa, but it's a winner. Right to size.

Grandpa:
> And, finally, Pip and Tommy, next time we meet we will not just talk about your client's room but will start to examine it in practical detail. Perhaps try a few body measurements. We'll ask it questions about its walls, windows, closet, heat, air conditioning, if any, and lighting.
>
> This was a great evening for us. And thanks, very much, for listening to an old man. Love ya.

Tommy, Pip And Carole:
> Grandma and Grandpa, ciao.

questions to explore

a. Who was Thomas Chippendale?

b. Who was George Hepplewhite?

Chapter 8

Close your eyes and "see" your territory.

Grandpa:
    Hi, kids. Good to see you. Today we're going to ask your client's room some questions.

Pip:
    If the room answers, I'm running out of here. I once saw a movie like that.

Grandpa:
    Let's go. We'll start with Tommy's client.

The threesome walks into Tommy's room.

Grandpa:
    Ready? Suppose we move some of this furniture away from the walls. Let's roll the bed out as far as we can.

Pip:
    Let us do it, Grandpa. It's too heavy and you'll hurt your back.

Grandpa:
    It's all right. This twin bed isn't that heavy. Look down at the base and notice it only consists of three pieces—a mattress on top of a box spring—set on a metal rack with wheels. The rack is called a bed frame. Quickly, how high do you think it all stands?

Tommy:
    I'd guess three spans. About twenty one inches.

Grandpa:
    Good estimate, Tommy. Also note that the frame is shorter than the box spring on one end. That's the front of the bed and the front of the frame. Now, what do you see in the back of the frame, Pip?

Pip:
    Two small pieces of metal with slits in it.

innerspring mattress and foundation

Grandpa:
    Those are flanges where you bolt a headboard on so as not to lean or sleep against the cold wall. The reason the front of the frame is shorter than the box spring is to prevent your rubbing your leg against it. And if you're not using a headboard it's a good idea to wrap some cloth around the flanges so they don't slam into the sheetrock of the wall and damage it.

Pip:
> That box spring and mattress is a body and an arm wide and about a body and two arms long. That makes it about forty inches wide and six feet and a span long.

Grandpa:
> That's great, Pip. The official width and length of a twin mattress and box spring is 39 inches by 75 inches. How did you know?

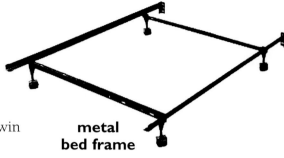
metal bed frame

Pip:
> I stretched out on mine last night and noticed there was about a span left at the foot of the mattress. I'm five foot six inches tall.

Tommy:
> This desk, here, is about forty inches long and about the height of our dining room table. Also, this chest is about thirty inches wide. A little more than an arm.

Grandpa:
> Fantastic! Did you guys stay up all last night? Don't answer. OK, now, carefully let's move the other few pieces a little away from the walls. Fine. Now what do you notice?

Pip:
> A couple of missing socks and two baseball cards.

Tommy:
> And a lot of dust. No wonder I'm always sneezing in here.

Grandpa:
> Ok, Tommy. Stand in the doorway of the room. One of the principles of good business is to know the "territory" you're going to work with. To get to know every inch. Every nook and cranny.

Pip:
> I've got it! It's his turf.

Grandpa:
> Exactly. For the first time you will "see" the room you have been looking at for years. You will "open" your eyes and get a feeling for the overall size and its individual parts. As an example, does this door you opened and closed a thousand times swing left or right? Does it swing in or out?

Tommy:
> It swings in and left against the wall.

Grandpa:
> Correct. Now what does it do to the length of that wall?

Tommy:
> It shortens it about an arm's length.

Pip:
> And doesn't allow furniture to be placed there.

Grandpa:
> Now what do we know about the shape of this territory? Is it a square or a rectangle?

Pip:
> It's not a square. Because if it were all the walls would be the same length. Right? And I can easily see that the wall that Tommy's on is much longer than the wall that the door hits on when opened.

Grandpa:
> So it's a rectangle. Two short parallel walls and two long parallel walls facing one another. Now, Tommy, while still standing in the doorway, scan the room with your eyes and "see" what those walls consist of and I'm not talking about sheetrock.

Tommy:
> I see....

Grandpa:
> Don't tell us. Just record it in your mind's eye. Go! One wall at a time from left to right. Good. Now do it once more. Fine. Now walk into the room, shut the door and sit down on the floor against it and close your eyes. Relax.

Pip:
> Careful, Grandpa, he's going to fall asleep on you.

Grandpa:
> Now, Tommy, with your eyes shut, tell us how you "picture" the room that you scanned. Start with the wall on your left where the door swings on to and call it "Wall B."

Tommy:
> Wall B is solid except for the door that swings in on it. Wall C has a window in the middle. Wall D is solid. Wall A has a closet on it. How's that?

Grandpa:
> Great first try. Pip is Tommy's description correct?

Pip:
> I think he did a great job but he made one boo-boo. He forgot the entrance door on Wall D. Right, Grandpa?

Grandpa:
> Is that right, Tommy? Tommy? Tommy? Open your eyes and get up. We're having the ice cream I brought along.

Tommy:
> Yes? I heard you. What flavor?

Grandpa:
> Pistachio. But let's finish up here, first. Now that the furniture is away from the walls let's take a good look at the encumbrances back there...structural blocks...that get in the way of furnishings. This time use your analysis notebook. Start with Wall B, Tommy. What do you find?

33

Tommy:
>Nothing. It's smooth.

Grandpa:
>Correct. Now face it and body measure it.

Tommy:
>It measures arm-body-arm plus arm-body. That's about 6 feet plus an arm-body. A total of about 9 feet.

Pip:
>Minus the room door that swings on to it. That's an arm wide. I measured mine last night.

Grandpa:
>That sounds on the button because a door in an apartment, outside of the front one, which is wider, usually measures a standard thirty inches. Now, both of you, draw a vertical line, label it Wall B and make the scale 1/2 inch to the foot. And since there are two half inches in one inch, then one inch represents two feet on your floor plan.
>   Then how long should the vertical Wall B line be?

Tommy:
>Four and a half inches, sir.

Pip:
>I'm proud of you, Tommy.

Grandpa:
>Pip, you try Wall C, the long wall with the window.

Pip:
>Here goes. The distance on either side of the window is about an arm-body and one shoe. That's about 54". And the window is about the same as the room door...one arm. That makes four and a half and four and a half. A total of 9 feet. Add the window, about another arm, and you have a total of approximately 12 feet. That's it for Wall C.

Tommy:
>Uh! Uh! Pip. Now you've made a boo-boo. You forgot to look on the floor. There's a baseboard heater under the window so all the furniture has to be moved out about five inches away from the wall. I know because I'm always picking things up back there.

Grandpa:
>He knows his territory, Pip. OK, Tommy, draw Wall C with the window in the middle at right angle to Wall B. Since the room is a rectangle you know the length of Wall D. Which now leaves us with Wall A that can't have a window because it is an inside wall. But what does it have?

Pip And Tommy:
>A closet and the door to the room.

Grandpa:
>And that's it, gang. You now have a rough sketch of Tommy's client's room. Four walls, one window, one closet, one entrance door and the heat. What two other factors are missing?

Tommy:
>The pistachio ice cream.

Grandpa:
>You're absolutely right, Tommy. Something cold. Except it's not ice cream but rather the air conditioning vent which is in the ceiling. A-n-d a most important utility, the electric wall sockets which have to be accessible. Mark them on the room plan.

Pip:
>Are we done for today, Grandpa?

Grandpa:
>Yes. You've studied the territory. Now you both have to draw a simple floor plan of your client's room based on your body measuring tape. Put each plan in an envelope and next time we meet we'll compare them with the original, exact measurements you put in the sealed envelopes weeks ago. Let's see how you guys measure up.

Tommy:
>I've got the whipped cream ready, Grandpa.

key terms

a. What is a "budget"?

b. What is "interest"?

questions to explore

a. Write three paragraphs about what you learned at the mall with only a two dollar budget.

b. How many industries did you discover there?

c. Could you qualify for a part-time job there? Doing what?

Chapter 9

*Needs. Wants. Wishes.
Sleep. Storage. Study.*

Grandma:
What time were the children supposed to show up, Pa?

Grandpa:
They'll be here in a bit. Pip called to say that she had chorus practice. Those kids are busier than a politician on the day before election. What with reports, computers, concerts and sport practice they need nine days in a week.

Grandma:
I get pooped just watching them run. I don't know how Carole does it with a full time career. Oh! I hear them on the walk.
   Come on in, children. Haven't seen you for over a month. How are you all doing?

Pip:
We were away with Mom for a couple of days and the snow was that high. Mom's fine and glad to be home. I guess we knocked her for a loop.

Tommy:
Here is my room plan, Grandpa. Hope it's right.

Pip:
Mine, too. Y'know? I didn't think my room was that large. I guess it's because I straightened it all out after I chucked a lot of the junk. My closet is also larger than Tommy's. It has two doors that slide in front of one another. I made a plan for the inside of that, too.

Grandpa:
You did? Maybe I'm doing something right, here.

Pip:
You didn't do anything wrong, Grandpa. Except that now you've got us excited about specifics in the room. It'll be a challenge to see how much I can get in there without piling it all over the floor and under my bed.

Tommy:
And I used the vacuum cleaner so my client stopped sneezing!

Grandma:
OK, first and last call for hot chocolate. You earned it.

Grandpa:
> I'd better sit down and have two Tylenol with the hot chocolate. All these welcomed reports are too much for my little old head.

Grandpa:
> Today we're just going to talk so get your "Joy of Analysis" book out. From here on you're on your own. No more telling you what columns to rule up and how many lines between listings.
> What I'd like to talk about are the needs, the wants and the wishes of your client.

Pip:
> Needs, wants and wishes, Grandpa?

Grandpa:
> Yes. Needs are absolute necessities. Wants are border line needs and wishes are border line wants. A few years ago a decorating magazine ran a survey among teenagers regarding their dream room and they were swamped with requests for ten foot round beds. Those are not needs or wants. They are day dreams.

Tommy:
> Especially in rooms like my client's. It's only about nine feet by thirteen feet.

Pip:
> The chests and desk would have to stand in the middle of the bed. That's only day dreaming stuff. Right, Grandpa?

Grandpa:
> I'll take another Tylenol, Ma.
> So-o-o, what do you think is a bedroom's must important need to properly serve the client?

Pip:
> A bed to sleep on.

Tommy:
> I guess that's why they call it a bedroom.

Grandpa:
> Correct. Beds come in, primarily, four sizes. I say, primarily, because there are sizes that do not have major distribution. The official sizes are twin, full, also called a double, queen and king. Got that? Good. And, in order, they measure in width: 39″, 54″, 60″ and 78″.

Tommy:
> And 75″ long you told us last time.

Grandpa:
> Right and wrong, Tommy. We were talking about the twin bed in your client's room. And that is 75″ long and so is the full or double bed. But the queen and king beds are 80″ long. So what size bed do you think will serve your client best?

Pip:
    Definitely a 39″ twin. Although I can't understand the name 'twin' considering only one person sleeps on it.

Grandpa:
    So we have the major need…sleep. And we serve that need with a bed. The next two major needs also start with the letter "S."

Tommy:
    How about space? We've got to put clothing away.

Pip:
    Wouldn't that be storage, Grandpa?

Grandpa:
    It sure would be storage and that would be served by chests with drawers or cabinets with doors. So far, so good. How about another "S"?

Pip:
    How about a place to do homework?

Grandpa:
    How about a place to study?

Tommy:
    That's it. The third "S." Sleep, storage and study areas.

Grandpa:
    And how would that need be served?

cheval mirror

Tommy:
    With a desk.

Pip:
    With bookcases.

Tommy:
    And a computer.

Grandpa:
    All those, if space and budget allow. But another major must is proper lighting. It is essential. It's an ingredient without which no room can function properly. I hope you indicated electrical outlets on your plans since lighting can be placed on a piece of furniture, on the floor, on a wall or on the ceiling.
    Now that we understand these basic needs let's think about "wants."

Pip:
    How about a CD player and speakers? And what do you call those long mirrors that tilt?

Grandpa:
    A cheval mirror.

Tommy:
   What about your aquarium and my telescope?

Pip:
   Do you think Mom will finally allow me a TV set or is that a wish instead of a want?

Grandpa:
   Knowing your Mom I would call that shot a wish. What do you think?

Pip and Tommy:
   Never!

Grandpa:
   I think you're right...and so is she. But I do think, if you plan your budget right, she might go for a VCR to be used with good judgment.

Pip:
   Well, then, how about a comfortable chair and a lamp standing next to it? I saw it in a decorating magazine. Want or wish, Grandpa?

Grandpa:
   I'd call that a fair wish. The problem, from experience, will be space allocation. In other words, all rooms have a given amount of floor space and you have to decide, one by one, what your priorities are. Loads of kids have tiny rooms that won't accommodate more than a bed, sometimes a smaller scaled one, a chest of drawers and a small desk. Your needs could be their wants and wishes.

Pip:
   You're right, Grandpa. I remember our other smaller apartment when Tommy and I were younger and we had the same bedroom. We had one bed that opened up into two.

Grandpa:
   That bed is called a hi-riser. One bed slips underneath the other and when needed can be pulled forward and up to sleep on.

bed with hi-riser

Tommy:
   I don't remember that. But what about my cousin, Alexander? Where's he going to sleep when he comes to visit from Michigan? I think that's a real need.

Grandpa:
   It's a legitimate one and you'll both have to face that problem when you plan out the actual pieces in your client's room. Remember, as I explained, every room, no matter how tiny, is eight feet high and so we'll see how we can stretch them by using "air space."

Pip:
   Is that why you had us scan all the walls with posters and pictures on them?

Grandpa:
That's absolutely right because if we want to put in layered beds that sleep two or three, or bookcases that stack on chests and desks, or shelves that attach to walls we need wall space. Posters, pictures, mirrors and collections are all important to create personal touches and warmth but you've got to take care of first things first: sleep, storage and study areas.

Tommy:
Gee! We sure covered a lot of territory. That's about everything.

Grandpa:
Not everything. If you think your mother is going to let you do homework on your new bed and break your back, you're mistaken. So don't you think it would be a good idea to include a desk chair among those needs?

Tommy:
You're right. And by the way, Grandpa, those special cookies that Grandma's neighbor makes are they needs, wants or wishes?

Grandma:
I heard you, Tommy. They're absolute needs and you don't have to worry about the budget. I'll meet you in the kitchen.

key terms

a. What is "veneer"?

questions to explore

a. What's the most valuable: reading, writing or math?

b. Do you do homework in front of the TV? Why?

Chapter 10

*How to enjoy shopping for home furnishings.
And make a salesperson your friend.*

Dear Pip and Tommy:

I've been called to speak at the American Society of Room Planners' regional meeting so I'll not be around next week to annoy you. Instead, I've decided to write you and give you time to absorb my words of wisdom. Next week we'll talk about them.

My name for this conversation was going to be: "How to make a salesperson your friend. And how to enjoy shopping for home furnishings." But I've changed my mind.

The name of this conversation is now reversed to: "How to enjoy shopping for home furnishings and make a salesperson your friend."

Why the switch? Because to make a salesperson your friend you first have to enjoy shopping for home furnishings and you can't enjoy shopping for home furnishings without knowing basic things about them...and yourself.

How? Right! by being prepared. Again, do your homework. Hm-m-m, do I detect that you're not groaning "Homework!" as loud as you did weeks ago when we first started this adventure in interior environment? Right? Great! And the reason you're not is because you've both done your homework (little by little) and know that it is the key to success in anything you undertake.

It's easy to make a salesperson your friend. Because not only do you want to buy things but, surprise! he or she wants to sell them to you. Very much so. That's how their rent is paid and food put on the table. In addition, if they sell day in and day out, they've got to enjoy it. Because, if they didn't it would show up, negatively, and people just wouldn't want to buy anything from them. Result? They'd be forced to try something else.

So, simply, the key to enjoying interior environment shopping is to learn all you can about what is available. To learn about the functions of the home furnishings you want to own and to learn about what quality of workmanship is worth, no matter how much you can afford to spend.

The rest is simple. Every salesperson will be your friend (will sincerely try to help you) because you appreciate what they are selling: what it does for you, what it should sell for and how to use and not abuse it.

By making any person's job more enjoyable and simpler you make a friend. That's Grandpa Mike's secret.

By the way, did you know that quality furniture tends to become more valuable with time? Ask your Aunt Sally, the designer, how much she pays for antiques and you'll be flabbergasted.

Think about this sermon and have a lot of questions when next Grandma and I hug you, because we're going furniture shopping. Thanks, again, for listening.

P.S.
I forgot. Before we go shopping together, do some shopping by yourselves...and not in a store. Have Mom collect weekend editions of two or three newspapers and magazine sections. Flip through them and cut out the furniture ads. If she can't get them easily, drop into your library for an hour and copy them.

This way you'll get familiar with the styles and values of different pieces that are featured and can think about which styles appeal more to you, personally, and why. Also start familiarizing yourselves with the furniture finishes (just light and dark) and the patterns and colors of fabrics.

Finally, with wood pieces pay attention to how the drawers are opened and how the pieces "sit" on the floor. Note if they are designed with legs or with solid bases down to the floor. Kisses to Mom.

Love,

Grandpa Mike

Grandpa Mike

key terms

a. What is a "couch potato"?

Chapter 11

The Couch Potato Fifty Percent Buying System.
Cars, carpenters and tuna fish salad sandwich friends.

Telephone rings in Carole Chalk's apartment.

Pip:

Hello, Grandpa? Yes, we're ready. We'll meet you downstairs in front of our apartment house in fifteen minutes. See ya.

Grandpa drives up to the apartment house in his little car: a yellow convertible with a roll top.

Grandpa:

All aboard!

Pip:

Gee! Grandpa! What a surprise! When did you get this nifty convertible?

Tommy:

I'll ride in the front.

Pip:

Oh! No! You won't. In the back, please.

Grandpa:

I bought it last fall, but just took it out of the shop. I had it checked out carefully, put on a fresh top and had it repainted. My friend owned it in Florida and just had it shipped to me. Isn't it great?

Pip:

Can I drive it, Grandpa, when I get my license?

Grandpa:

Maybe. We'll see what kind of a driver you'll be, Pip. A license only allows you to drive a vehicle. It doesn't mean that you've been certified as being careful with the car, other people or your own life. So, we'll see.
   Do you have any questions about the letter I wrote you?

Tommy:

We talked it over and we both had the same question, sir.

Grandpa:

And that is?

Pip:

Why do we have to make sure that a salesperson is going to be our friend? After all, it's our money we're spending and shouldn't he or she be pleasing us?

Tommy:
That's right. After all, the salesperson is being paid and the company makes money on what we buy.

Grandpa:
Super question, gang. You've been thinking. The truth is that this is all a sort of Grandpa Mike buying philosophy. I even try this "friend" thing when I'm having my car repaired or choose a carpenter or even when I order a tuna salad sandwich on whole wheat. You see, all service people are really salespersons. In each case, even the tuna salad sandwich, they know (or should know) more about what they are selling than I do. They are on the firing line.

Tommy And Pip:
Even with the tuna sandwich?

Grandpa:
Yes, even with the tuna sandwich. You see they know if the whole wheat bread, which I usually order, is fresh. That's why they always ask "Do you want it toasted?" because whole wheat doesn't sell as often as white or rye and therefore, is rarely as fresh and, usually, could use toasting. But I like it without toasting. Fresh.

So when buying, I need and you need a real friend who knows the score. One who we can trust and will help us avoid making costly or unpleasant mistakes.

Pip:
Wow! Grandpa. If you need a friend in a restaurant when spending a few dollars then you certainly need one in a furniture store when you could be spending a hundred.

Grandpa:
How about more like a thousand? Did you read the advertisements I suggested?

Tommy:
We sure did. It was fun.

Pip:
Especially when you're not actually spending the money.

Grandpa:
That's the point, kids. When you are spending it, it's not always fun. It's a very serious matter that can reach into thousands of dollars, even for smaller rooms. People who have no "friends" to help them really get frightened. And I don't blame them. It's a scary adventure because most people don't plan.

Pip:
We know. They don't do their homework.

Tommy:
And don't have a space plan or know how much to spend.

Grandpa:
Or have a friend they can trust. Someone who is recommended to them that is knowledgeable, thorough, pleasant and forthright.

Pip:

    Forthright, Grandpa?

Grandpa:

    Yes, forthright. He or she not only has to know what to recommend but what not to recommend and why. And only by your politely helping with the basic facts of room plan, needs and approximate budget can they make an intelligent decision. You've got to know your territory and lay it out for your "friend."

Pip:

    Well, Grandpa, we know a little about our client's territory: Like the room size, the needs, wants and wishes but we don't know what things look like or cost.

Grandpa:

    Right. And that's the reason I had you clipping out ads. To get a fundamental idea what furnishings look like and basically are worth. Very basic. And that's why Grandpa Mike invented the "Fifty-Percent Couch Potato Buying System." You never leave your couch. You never get tired or have aching feet. All you have to do is take the prices in the ads and add fifty percent to them. That will make them budget-realistic for the version you are going to buy. Do you know what that means?

Tommy:

    I think so. It means if something is advertised for $100 you're probably going to spend fifty percent more and…

Pip:

    That makes it $150. Wow-e-e! Tommy saw a bunk bed advertised for $200 so that makes it $300 for budgeting purposes.

Tommy:

    And it said "mattresses not included."

Grandpa:

    So you see that the more you know before you start out looking and talking to salespersons the better equipped you will be to choose what is needed and affordable. The better you'll be equipped to ask questions, give answers and choose salespersons who really want to help you do a good job.

    Well, here we are. Don't forget your "Joy" books? By the way, Wittnower's Furniture is a good place to start looking. They're friends of mine and the family has been in business for three generations. From experience, I trust them, respect them and appreciate their knowledge and service. Let's go take a general look!

Pip:

    Do you think it might rain, Grandpa?

Grandpa:

    Not with that bright sunshine. But, you two guys can have the fun of pulling the top down, anyway. Oh! Grandma's cookies are in the glove compartment. We can all have one or two before we go inside.

Chapter 12

Space planning with "Push-Together-Systems."
Space planning with "Selective Eclectic" complements.

Grandpa pulls into Wittnower's Furniture parking field.

Grandpa:
Before we go in, kids, I'd like to explain a few things about what I'm trying to accomplish. Today is the beginning of the end of your formal sessions with me. However, it also is the beginning of your examining, touching and recognizing furniture for your client's room.

Starting today you will make notes about what's available: in color, known as finish, function and cost and you will try to picture in your mind's eye how they would look in a particular room. With your body measuring system you will approximate their size and then you will enter the exact size in width, height and depth, as checked out by your tape measure.

One more thing. I'm very proud of you two, so I expect you to act as polite adults. Any questions?

Pip:
Yes, Grandpa. When will we pick the exact things that we like and think will fit best into our project?

Grandpa:
After one more round of checking ads, a visit on your own to a department store and a return trip here. It's just as important to learn what you don't think fits properly into your project as what does. Let's go! A-n-d ....

Pip and Tommy:
Keep your eyes open.

Grandpa:
Luv ya. From here on in, you're on your own.

Grandpa, Pip and Tommy enter the store. They are approached by a store employee.

Store Employee:
May I help you?"

Grandpa:
Yes, please. We have an appointment with Mr. Wittnower.

Store Employee:
Which one, please?

Grandpa:
Oh! Senior, please.

Store Employee:
And your names, please?

Grandpa:

Pip, Tommy and Grandpa Mike.

Mr. Wittnower shows up.

Wittnower:

Mike! It's wonderful seeing you. Are these the "special grandchildren" that you told me about?

Grandpa:

Very special, Neil. This young lady is Pip and this is her brother, Tommy.

Wittnower:

It's a pleasure meeting you. Mike has told me all about you two and a lot about your client projects. I want to thank you for coming to Wittnower's. And, now, how can we help you?

Pip:

Well, sir, we're not making any decisions, today, but we'd like to look around at furniture that teenagers use…and not too expensive because we've got a budget to fit.

Tommy:

Yes, sir. And our rooms are not too big, either.

Wittnower:

Well, Pip and Tommy, let me take you to the second floor. We have a whole department we've labeled the "I Wish Collection" that we think you'll appreciate. It showcases complete groupings by various manufacturers. In addition, our staff has set aside a section that we call "Selected Eclectic" in which they've blended pieces from one collection with pieces and accents from others.

I think they did a superb job. In fact, they're now in the process of doing "Selected Eclectic" themes for our dining rooms and master bedrooms on the first floor. Let's take the elevator up.

Pip:

How long have you been in this business, Mr. Wittnower?

Wittnower:

I'm third generation. My grandfather started the business in 1939, my father joined it after World War II and college under the G.I. Bill and I'm here, full time, since 1976. I say "full time" because I've really been here forever. Like all retail family children, sweeping and being a go-fer in the warehouse or helping drivers make deliveries after school or on weekends is part of the growing up process.

Tommy:

That's a long time!

Wittnower's second floor.

Tommy:

How big is this place, sir?

Wittnower:

We have two floors of approximately 23, 000 square feet each for display and a 50,000 square feet warehouse downtown on the river front. Here is our "I Wish Collection." We show sixteen groupings, some in two finishes.

I'll leave you be. Mike, if you need me just pick up one of our Customer Inquiry phones on the walls. Although I have a hunch that you know these groupings better than I do. It's a pleasure meeting you, Pip and Tommy.

Mr. Wittnower leaves.

Pip:

I think I like your friend, Grandpa. He seems to know his products and I think I'd trust his judgment.

Tommy:

Looks like he's done his homework for a long, long time.

Grandpa:

Longer then you think. Well, let's get started. First, I think it might be a good idea for the three of us to separate and go our own way in the "I Wish Collection." As you roam around, think of each manufacturer's group as a cast of a play. The main character or the lead is the chest of drawers. That determines the theme and character of the group. Then makeup and costuming is added...the finish, the trimmings, the detailing and the hardware (or grips) to open the drawers

Tommy:

Makeup, Grandpa? What about boys' groups?

Grandpa:

No difference. Could be the equivalent of longer sideburns, a beard, heavy eyebrows, a dimple or a wrinkled forehead. Or an earring, like in a pirate play.

Pip:

Where do the beds and the desks fit in?

Grandpa:

Right alongside like a supporting cast. The bed usually has super-special lines of its own and tries to steal the spotlight. The desk (with chair) is the serious character and is always busy doing something like writing letters or keeping records. The mirrors, the bookcases and the shelves form the background chorus. How's that for an imaginative presentation, Pip?

Pip:

Unbelievable, Grandpa! You just were carried away like I was with my first dream room. Remember? Any way you look at it, it was a Pip. How's that, Grandpa?

Grandpa:

Super! I got a bit carried away but I think my dramatic comparison will hold water before we're finished. Wait and see. In the meantime, let's start looking and taking notes in the "I Wish Collection" area. Then we'll tackle the "Selective Eclectic" section.

Tommy:

OK, I'm off.

Grandpa:
> Oh! One last thought. While you're scouting, keep an eye peeled for the finishes. We'll just call them white, light, medium or dark. Also note the height of the various storage chests. There could be as many as four different ones. And to make sure that we will be talking about the same group, check the hang-tags on one piece for a group name or number.
>
> We're off!

key terms

a. What is the "G.I. Bill"?

b. Did anyone in your family use it?

questions to explore

a. Would you like to own a furniture store? Why?

b. What do you think of Grandpa Mike's tuna fish salad sandwich story? Does it make sense?

Chapter 13

Looking at furniture for the 100th time and seeing it for the first time with your eyes "open".

Wittnower's Furniture

Tommy:
Where's Grandpa, Pip?

Pip:
Right behind you stretched out on the other side of that recliner chair.

Grandpa:
Just relaxing here. And that's where I'm going to stay while I listen to the two of you reviewing what you saw. Go ahead and make believe I'm not here. Remember, I said you're on your own.

Tommy:
OK, sir. Wasn't it fun, Pip, going through all those rooms?

Pip:
Sure was. Especially the way they have each room fixed up as if a kid were living in it. Did you like anything for your client, Tommy?

Tommy:
Well, after looking around I think my client would like something in one of the lighter wood finishes. Not painted white ones, they're too girly-girly for me. I'd rather have the light brown ones that have the lines of the original tree showing.

Pip:
You know I'm not girly-girly but I do like that group with the white paint because I've been living with all the hand-me-down dark stuff, forever. But if you look, closely, it's not like the mica group in the corner that's pure white. This one sort of looks like it has brush marks running through it.

Tommy:
Did you notice that the sizes of the pieces are pretty much the same in all the sets. Here take a look in my "Joy" book: a chest with three drawers is 30″ wide, one with six drawers, three and three alongside one another, is 44″ wide.

Pip:
And they're all 18″ inches deep and 30″ high, including the 4-drawer desk which is also 44″ wide. That's why the same bookcase fits on a desk and a double dresser.

Tommy:
Double dresser? How did you know the three-and three-drawer chest is called a double dresser?

50

Pip:

It's simple, Tommy. It's written on the price tag. And the chest with three drawers is called a bachelor chest. I'll bet you loved the computer desk with the built-in sliding tray for a computer keyboard.

Tommy:

And I'll bet that you flipped over that canopy bed with the high posts. It looks like the one you sketched for your dream room.

Pip:

How did you know that it was a 4-poster canopy bed?

Tommy:

Simple. It was an ad in last Sunday's Tribune newspaper. The one I cut out.

Pip:

I did flip but it doesn't make any sense, anymore, Tommy. It'll fit in my client's room but it's too bulky, to my eye.

Tommy:

Pip, did you notice how the pieces push together in most of the groupings?

Pip:

I sure did. But I also noticed others they had standing by themselves that couldn't be pushed together. Like the ones in my client's room now. I'll have to ask Grandpa about those.

Tommy:

Y'know, Pip, it's not easy to choose the right bed. I think there must have been at least five or six different kinds. One was a bunk bed that could sleep two… one on the top and one on the bottom. And one could even sleep three… one on the top twin size and two on the bottom full size bed. Cousins Alex and Lauren would have a ball when they'd visit.

And did you see the bunk bed with the chest slipped in under the high top bunk?

Pip:

Can't beat those for a pajama sleep over party. And did you see the different sizes in chests? 2-drawer, 3-drawer, 6-drawer and others with doors. I even spotted the armoire and the lingerie chest that got me to sign up for Grandpa Mike's lessons. At least, I now know what they call them.

Tommy:

Look here, Pip. I drew some of the handles that open the drawers and doors. Wooden ones and iron ones. Every shape you can dream of. It's endless.

Pip:

I think that the people that do these settings must have a lot of fun. You know, Tommy, now that we've really touched the furnishings I can't wait to see the "Selective Eclectic" section. Shall we check in with Grandpa Mike?

captain's bed

Tommy:
>We'd better. I'm getting hungry.

Both:
>Come out, come out wherever you are, Grandpa.

Grandpa:
>Well, I'm really delighted with you two. As I listened to your observations I was honestly pleased how you really kept your eyes open. Great!
>
>I'm also delighted that you're anxious to see the "Selective Eclectic" section because I am, too. However, before we move on I want to add to some of your observations.
>
>First, regarding the white finishes. When furniture is sprayed, the whole piece, or case, as it is called, is solid white. But then the finishers know how to wipe off just the right amount to catch in the natural grain of the wood. The contemporary suites, meaning the straight line ones with flat drawers, use that technique. The traditional groups, those with carved legs that lift them off the floor and with shaping on the drawers, tend to use a brushed finish and have brass handles. They're not iron, Tommy.
>
>Mica groupings are, generally, simple boxes and the colors are usually solid opaque or simulated wood grains. But you can have fun with strips, pulls or drawers of contrasting colors. In white they are feminine, by design. The color does it. If they were red or chocolate they'd have less chance of being a specific gender. Got it?

sleigh bed

Pip:
>I think so, Grandpa.

Grandpa:
>This is really an oversimplified way of explaining style and finishes and if your Aunt Sally, the designer, heard me she'd have an indigestion attack. But, in my book, it's a basic way for beginning space planners to become aware of and to appreciate the depth and variety available for interior environments.
>
>It's getting late and I think we're all getting hungry, so let's not delay any further because I am just as anxious as you two are to see the "Selective Eclectic" section. I'll finish my shpiel later.
>
>Let's get going, again, and please keep using your "Joy" books. It's impossible to remember everything you see. And, once again, you guys do the talking and I'll do the listening. Of course, I'll always have the last word.

Both:
>Don't we know it.

Grandpa, Pip and Tommy head for the "Selective Eclectic" department.

Pip:
> Grandpa! Tommy! Just look at this department! It looks just like those pictures in color that Mom showed us last week in her decorating magazine. I love it.

Tommy:
> It sure makes a lot of difference when you mix different ideas.

Pip:
> It's not just ideas, Tommy. It's different design ideas working together. That's fun. The clothing stores do it every day so you and your friends don't all end up wearing the same things. They call it "Mix and Match."

Grandpa:
> That's what eclectic is all about. Choosing complementary items to create a fresh idea. Here, Pip, look as this free-standing dresser from the other department.....

Pip:
> That's it, Tommy. That's the one I was talking to you about. You see you can't push it next to another piece, like a desk, for instance. Instead of being flush, it has an edge on both ends that hangs over instead of being flush. What did you call it, Grandpa?

Grandpa:
> Free-standing. It's also a bit higher and bit deeper than the flush pieces. Now, where was I?

Tommy:
> I wrote it down. Something about creating a fresh idea.

Grandpa:
> Right. This furniture manufacturer makes a matching mirror, and it's handsome, too, but the store designer decided to use a gold framed mirror from another grouping.
> It's like wearing a plaid scarf with a solid color beret. Two good ideas to create a third one.

loft bed

Tommy:
> And look here. This bed between these two chests doesn't match them either. It looks like the sofa in our den with all those pillows on it.

Grandpa:
> That's a daybed, Tommy, and it's made of wicker, which comes from countries in the Pacific Rim. The basic color is tan but it's been painted white. Very feminine. It also is made with a hi-riser hidden under it.

Pip:
> That's it, Tommy. The kind of bed we used to sleep on in the old apartment. You pull it out and up.

Tommy:
> Look at this chocolate colored mica bed. It just has a board under the mattress. No box spring.

Grandpa:
> It's a platform bed. No headboard. It also can be had with a long drawer under it for storage. Notice that the long side is against the wall like your sofa in the living room. And how do you like those white wood chests on either side?

Pip:
> Gee! Grandpa I think my client would like some arrangement like that. The room would be more spacious and, perhaps, I can fit in that chair and footstool that I saw in the decorating magazine. I think they called it an ottoman.

Grandpa:
> It is an ottoman. An overstuffed footstool that gets it's name from the founder of the Turkish Ottoman Empire. His name was Othman. There's a touch of history here, Pip.
> And some day you can do a report for a history project by researching the historic backgrounds of such designs as English Oak, French Provincial, American Shaker and Spanish Mission furniture. I know you'd love it.

Tommy:
> Look at this bed! The headboard is covered in cloth and the bedspread matches it. I like it but it seems it would be better for a girl's room.

Pip:
> That's no problem, Tommy. All you have to do is change the flowered fabric to a rugged looking fabric like a tweed.

Grandpa:
> Where did you get that idea?

Pip:
> From clothing, sir. Tommy has a pair of trousers in tweed. Cloth is cloth whether it's on your back or on your bed.

Grandpa:
> That's super, Pip. In fact, research has shown that colors and textures in apparel trends are soon followed in home furnishings. I guess the consumer's eye get's to feel comfortable with it and adopts it to a room setting.

Pip:
> I remember your pointing that out when we were talking about colors. You said that there really was nothing new in color combinations.

Grandpa:
> You're right. That's exactly what I said. By the way, Tommy, you said before that Mom showed you and Pip some color pictures of room settings in a decorating magazine. Has she shown you a lot of them?

Tommy:
> She has a pile of them. Never noticed her reading so many before.

Pip:

She's also been collecting interior environment and furniture ads, too. And I know why. I think she's been doing her homework.

Tommy:

Homework? What for?

Pip:

For the Supreme Family Court session. She knows we're going to present our client's room plan and budget and she wants to be prepared to judge them. Our Mom never does anything half baked. She even helps all our neighbors with their taxes.

Grandpa:

Well, kids, that's a good note to end on. How about taking another ten minutes to jot down the prices of things you have seen here because Mom is going to go on an expedition with you two next weekend. Probably to two more stores. And that will be D-Day for you and your clients.

Tommy:

Sir, can we eat? Because if we don't I'll never make it to the Supreme Family Court session.

Grandpa:

You know, Tommy, I think I'd rather furnish your client's room than feed you. Let's check the price tags and go downstairs and say "Thank you" to Mr. Wittnower.

key terms

a. What is "opaque"?

questions to explore

a. Did you ever see something with your eyes closed? If yes, what?

Chapter 14

Space Planner's Room Plan.
Whose is it? It's really the client's.

Grandpa:
Well, it's D-Day kids. Let's talk about the space planner room plans. Who is going to volunteer to be first?

Pip:
You should, Tommy, because every time I jump in first on the front seat of Mom's car or run ahead in the movie theater to buy the tickets you try to beat me to it. So here's your chance to be Numero Uno.

Tommy:
OK with me. Here goes. First of all, sir, here are the measurements of my room, according to the Body-Measurement-Tape.

Grandpa:
And here are the measurements you took with a measuring tape. Still safe and sound in your sealed envelope. And the winner is, of course, the sealed envelope measurements, which are 10 feet by 13 feet. However, the Body-Measurement-Tape numbers run a close second: 9 feet by 12 feet, leaving you, Tommy, with about a ten percent margin of error. A foot in each direction. I think that's a terrific percentage for a first try.

Pip:
Can I read mine off, Grandpa?

Grandpa:
Go right ahead, Pip.

Pip:
The Body-Measurement-Tape numbers are 12 feet by 16 feet. So how did I do?

Grandpa:
Couldn't be better. The sealed numbers are 12 feet by 15 feet. Bingo! Just a bit extra on the length. Good work guys.

Pip:
I've been thinking about the system, Grandpa and I'm sure I can come in almost on the button every time. It's really simple because I've tried it.

Grandpa:
Oh?

Pip:
You just have to be careful when you record the original arm and finger measurements. You have to make sure they are fully stretched out. Same thing for your hand span. And then you must take care that you do the same thing when you use them.

Tommy:
>And don't forget to locate your hip bone when you take your waist height. I find that the spot right on top is the easiest one to find every time.

Grandpa:
>Another item to be careful to note are the ledges under windows and the frames around doors and windows. They take up space, too. I must say, that for two amateurs you've certainly got the Body-Measurement-Tape down pat. The fun of it all is to get it fixed in your mind's eye. Practice will do it. Now let's see your client's room layout, Tommy.

>**Tommy lays it out on the table.**

Grandpa:
>Tell us about it, Tommy.

Tommy:
>First, I made a list of my client's needs. Sleep, study and storage. In sleep he wanted a bunk bed. In study he needed a lot of desk place for his computer. In storage he would be happy with whatever I fit in.

Pip:
>Whatever you fit in?

Tommy:
>That's right, Pip. I'm the Space Planner and when I looked over what he has to store away I noticed that most of the things could be hung up in a closet. They were bulky.

Grandpa:
>Go on, Tommy. You're on a roll.

Tommy:
>When we went shopping with Mom, I saw one of the same groups that we saw at Mr. Wittnower's store. So I talked it over with my client and he liked it, too. It had a wood grain finish that wasn't too dark.

Pip:
>That's interesting, Tommy.

Tommy:
>I also learned from the measurements of the room that my client could use a corner desk, which goes around a corner, with a computer desk in the Push-Together-Systems. It would make a giant desk. Well, this grouping had them both. The other need that my client has is a two level bed. A bunk bed. And this one even had a two level bed that comes with storage drawers under the bottom bed.

Grandpa:
>That makes it a three-level one.

Tommy:
>Yes, I know. I was thinking vertical and I explained that to Mom when we went looking. Now the only thing that was left was to figure out how many chests I could fit bookcase hutches on. How did I do, Grandpa?

Grandpa:

    I can't believe it, Tommy! It's a great job. What do you think, Pip?

Pip:

    I can't believe it, either! Do you think Mom's budget will stand all of that?

Grandpa:

    Frankly, I don't know. We never discussed the numbers. But I do see some parts of Tommy's plan that can be shaved without damaging the basic needs. How about leaving all the questions and comments for the end. OK, Pip. You're on.

Pip:

    Before I present my plan, Grandpa, I want to tell you a bit about my shopping experience with Mom. It's sort of your tuna fish on whole wheat story.

Grandpa:

    Sounds interesting, Pip. Let's hear it.

Pip:

    Well, when we went with Mom to the other two stores she chose I wasn't very happy. I was disappointed for a few reasons. When I collected the ads from the store on Carlton Avenue the pieces looked real good to me but when I saw the actual furniture it seemed tinny.

Tommy:

    Tinny?

Pip:

    Yes. The drawers didn't close tightly and one of the pulls had a screw missing. Everything sort of rattled around. That sort of turned me off because those were the problems of some of my hand-me-down furniture. No sense spending Mom's hard-earned money and ending up with the same problems.

Tommy:

    Gee! Pip! I'm glad you're my sister. I mean that.

Pip:

    In the second store on the corner of Walton and Scott Boulevard I felt a lot better. They really had great-looking groupings but they didn't have enough to choose from. At least not for me. I guess I was spoiled at the Wittnower store by their Selected Eclectic section. As soon as I saw it, I liked the idea that not everything matched. So Mom took me over there.

    Now here is my plan. I hope you guys like it.

Pip lays out her client plan.

Grandpa:

    Very interesting, Pip. Tommy?

Tommy:

    M-m-m-m.

Grandpa:

    Let's hear it, Pip.

Pip:

I want my client's room to be a knockout the moment you walk in. So I put the bed on the wall that faces the door. And the bed is an iron daybed that has a hi-riser bed hidden under it that can be pulled out for a sleepover guest. That was one of her wants.

Tommy:

Like the one we had when we were kids!

Pip:

Right, Tommy. Then I placed a 44″ double dresser on each side of the bed to act as night tables for a lamp and radio. Over one of the dressers I hung a white, oval wicker mirror to blend with the brushed white finish of the furniture and over the other there's a bookcase hutch for her book collection. So that fills three needs: sleep, guest and storage for clothes and books. Unlike Tommy's client, my client has loads of soft underclothes that need drawer space.

Tommy:

Wow! Grandpa! My sister sure did her homework! Now how about the study need, Pip?

Pip:

There it is. The desk and chair are on the opposite wall where it's nice and quiet without a window to daydream through. Over the desk I hung shelves for how-to computer manuals and software. And, Grandpa, that box drawn next to the desk is a cabinet to hold my client's music collection. I need your help to find the exact style.

Grandpa:

I don't know about you, Tommy, but after that professional space planner presentation I could use a hot drink and a secret formula cookie or two. Pip, it's great! I'm very proud of you.

Tommy:

I was so interested I forgot I was getting hungry.

Grandpa:

Into the kitchen, kids. We'll finish up after a twenty minute break. Maybe Grandma left some ice cream, too.

Grandpa:

OK. Let's go back to Tommy's plan. I like the way it swings around the room with the corner desk in the upper left corner. It's the best of the three usable corners in the room. Had Tommy used the upper right corner, the bunk bed would have ended up either overlapping the closet or it would have faced you as you walk in and that would have been clumsy. Like walking into a wall.

Tommy:
>I know that, sir, because this is not my first plan. It's my third.

Grandpa:
>Next. You have to carefully recheck your measurements on the window wall because if you're a few inches out of the way, your hutch is going to be smack in front of the window and that's a no-no. Anyway, I think that the room would appear larger if the hutch went on the other bachelor chest, in the corner. Second, you also have to recheck the distance between the end of the bunk bed and the bachelor chests in the corner. If it's less than two feet it will be difficult to open the drawers. Now what kind of a chair are you using for the desks, Tommy?

Tommy:
>The one that matches looks fine. And I sat in it, too. Why?

Grandpa:
>What do you think, Pip?

Pip:
>I see what you're driving at, Grandpa. I think that he should use an office type chair on wheels so that he can move it easily back and forth between the corner desk and computer desk.

Grandpa:
>Anything else you want to talk about, Tommy?

Tommy:
>Yes, sir. My client's room has an old fashioned lamp hanging down from the ceiling, on a chain. I think it's awful but I don't know what to do about it. What do you suggest?

Grandpa:
>Good question. I noticed that Pip's client has a similar problem. First, it's not called an old-fashioned lamp. It's a lighting fixture and it does have to be changed. I would like track lighting which is a simple strip into which a metal shade is slipped that can slide back or forth. One track can have two shades or spots, as they're called, that can be directed to the desk area or the bed area. However, some sort of lamp will still be needed next to the bed or clipped on to it.

Pip:
>I know that style, Grandpa. I see it in stores all the time. I think it would be fine for Tommy's client but I know my client wouldn't be happy. It's too cold looking. I'd rather place one lamp on the dresser where the head of the bed is and another different one where the desk is.

Grandpa:
>What kind of desk are you using, Pip?

Pip:
>I was waiting for you to ask. It's a home-office one in a different finish. A dark finish. The second store had it.

Tommy:
>Sounds expensive to me. Did you check the price tag?

Pip:

I did. It's not cheap but if you notice I only have two major pieces of furniture in my plan so I was watching the budget. And I also eliminated the chair and ottoman and standing lamp that I saw in the magazine. Remember?

Grandpa:

I remember. Two more things to remember when the Supreme Family Court starts to ask questions: One, know exactly where the wall outlets are located. Two, get your prices together. Three, know how many square yards of carpeting your plans will take. Do you know how to figure that, approximately?

Tommy:

I never thought about it, Grandpa, but one thing I do know is that there are three feet in a yard. So if my room is ten feet by twelve feet then it is 3-1/3 yards by 4 yards. I think that's about thirteen and a third yards.

Pip:

Which makes my twelve feet by fifteen feet 4 yards by 5 yards. That's twenty yards.

Grandpa:

Great! The only trouble is that carpeting doesn't come in single yard widths. It comes in twelve and fifteen feet widths and if your room is 12 feet 2inches you have to use a fifteen foot width, right? And that causes carpet waste that you must pay for. Which is why all fine carpet stores have experienced mechanics who measure rooms exactly- very exactly and know how to lay them out.

Tommy:

So-o-o?

Grandpa:

So for the purpose of this project's budget let's figure your room, Tommy, as being 12 by 15 and yours, Pip, as being 15 by 15. And that makes your room, Tommy, take......

Tommy:

Twenty yards.

Pip:

And mine twenty-five yards.

Grandpa:

And it also makes our space planning session complete. Thanks a million. I loved every minute. Ciao.

key terms

a. What is a "corporate stock"?

questions to explore

a. Does your family ever have Supreme Family Court sessions? Do you think it's a good idea?

Chapter 15

Grandpa Mike's Unbelievable Up-and-Down Bedroom Decorating System. Wow-e-e!

Carole Chalk's apartment. Door bell rings.

Tommy:
I've got it, Pip. It's got to be Grandma Anita and Grandpa Mike.

Tommy opens the door.

Tommy:
Hi, kids.

Grandma:
Kids?

Tommy:
Isn't that what you always say? Oh! I thought I'd be funny.

Grandma:
Love ya a million, anyway. Here, Tommy, put this bag in the refrigerator. How did you make out in the math team tryouts?

Tommy:
I sure was scared. You should have heard the other guys in the group. They were real good.

Grandma:
Don't you worry about it. It's an honor just to be chosen for the tryouts and I'm sure that you rated pretty high. The trying is just as important as the winning. Besides you've also been pretty busy with this room planning project of yours.

Tommy:
I know. But I still would love to make that team. Pip! The other kids are here.

Pip:
Hello, folks. Tommy is having one of his funny days. What made you call and make this special trip, Grandpa?

Grandpa:
Two things. First, I want to blitz you through Grandpa Mike's Up-and-Down Bedroom Decorating System, just in case the Supreme Family Court should ask a question or two. And, secondly, I'd like to see your closets again. If it's OK with you guys.

Pip:
OK here. I've kept it in good order since you were here last.

Tommy:
Anytime.

Grandpa:

Here's my system. It's short and sweet. I've learned from experience that most people are troubled about knowing where to start the finishing touches of a bedroom. The decorating. So in their anxiety they grab the first flooring or sheet or window treatment that's on sale and then end up with having to dovetail the rest of the room with it. That could become a wasteful dead end.

Pip:

How did you know I was worried about that?

Grandpa:

It's a natural progression. Decorators are always hearing from their clients about the beautiful, little chest that they inherited from a distant aunt and now want to decorate a whole room around it. That's a backwards point to start from. So here's Grandpa Mike's ingenious, cost-effective, bedroom decorating plan that suggests where you start and where you go from there. In my book, the key place to start with is the bed covering. It could be a bedspread or a comforter or, even, a sheet. That is the launching platform for the whole room.

Pip:

Does that mean a print or pattern of some sort?

Grandpa:

Yes. It could be a flowered design or stripe or geometric pattern. You can easily see that would set the color scheme for the entire room.

Tommy:

And then?

Grandpa:

Then you work your way up and down. From the comforter, let's say, you can choose one of the colors for the carpeting or the area rug. It could be one of the pattern colors or the background. That's the down move.

Tommy:

Remember that bed I told you about at Wittnower's Furniture with the fabric headboard? That means you could choose a solid color or the same pattern for it, right?

Grandpa:

Right. And, to keep your cost down, for a matching fabric you could use a matching bedsheet and cut it up. Again, pals, as usual, you have to do your homework and check to see if that connection is available before you spend one nickel of your mother's hard earned money.

Pip:

Now I can see where you're heading with your system, Grandpa. First you choose a patterned bed covering, then you choose a companion, like the background color, for the carpeting. Then you can work your way up to the upholstered headboard, if you like an upholstered one, and further up to the wall paint.

Tommy:

Outside of the carpeting it's the old think vertical system that we used for furniture.

Grandma:

Am I really hearing all this? Or is this some sort of recording?

Grandpa:
You're hearing it, alright, Grandma. These two friends of ours have done their homework and, more important, have found ways to use their common sense in this education adventure.

Pip:
I like it! I like it! Now what about the windows?

Tommy:
I don't think my client would like all kinds of fluffy stuff on his window.

Grandpa:
Window treatments, as they are called, are a cinch because there are so many inexpensive ones to choose from. Here I brought this pamphlet along for you to take a look at. If Tommy's client doesn't like fluffy stuff all he needs to do is choose an aluminum blind. They come vertical, with strips in the length or horizontal with the strips from side to side.

Pip:
And, I saw one at my friend Patty's house that comes with a rod on the side that you can twist to adjust the light coming in.

Grandpa:
And the best part is that they come in a slew of solid covers so you can match the wall paint.

I recommend this for your client, Tommy, because it will also make his room appear larger by seemingly blending into the wall. That's another room stretching trick that we talked about at the very beginning of this project. And, by the way, loads of clients make the mistake of painting the wood trim around their windows, closets and doors in contrasting colors or wood stain and that's a boo! boo! in my book. They're only accentuating the negative.

What do you think your client might like, Pip?

Pip:
Well, I have to think it out with her but my first reaction is to also go with the horizontal blinds. But I'd like to add some print at the windows.

Grandpa:
That's a cinch to do because many of the bed covering packages include draperies and valances–those are the ruffles across the top. The draperies usually are long ones for a whole window and you can cut them down to go just past the window sill. Or you can use just the valances.

Grandma:
If you or a friend ever took a sewing course in home economics you can take the fabric that you cut off the draperies and sew it into decorative pillows for the bed or tack it, upholster, onto a board you can mount across the top of your window. It's called a cornice.

Grandpa:
Thanks, Grandma. It's also shown here in this how-to pamphlet. Now how come I haven't heard the million dollar question?

Tommy:
> I've got it. Suppose your client doesn't want any patterns? Just something plain like a light tan comforter.

Grandpa:
> The basics are still the same. You choose a solid color for the bedcovering and then proceed with the Up-and-Down-System. Of course you can have everything in a monotone...one color or shades of one color. To me that's kind of a no-pizzazz track for a young person's bedroom.
>
> Then again, you can choose a low-key plaid in beiges or a woven pattern for the flooring and add a striped wallpaper for an accent...and not necessarily on all walls. Of course, you should take into consideration the finish of the furniture you've chosen. If it isn't framed by the wall color it just disappears.

Tommy:
> That's a lot of homework.

Grandpa:
> Yes and no, this time. Common sense and a method of procedure makes it easy. Think. How many finishes does a ready-made, furniture grouping come in?

Pip:
> One or two from what we saw.

Grandpa:
> How many colors and patterns is a given, ready-made bedcovering available in? Maybe three and mostly in one. And how many wallpapers and paint colors are easily available?

Pip:
> When we went looking for paint chips I saw hundreds just in one store.

Grandpa:
> So, Grandpa Mike's Up-and-Down Bedroom Decorating System therefore makes sense: Number One: furniture and finish. Two: bedcovering. Three: flooring. Four and Five: wall colors and window treatments. And, finally, not to forget all the pictures and photos and banners and teddy bears and floating fish that we inventoried. That's your personality touch.

> **Door bell rings**

Grandma:
> I'll get it, kids. It's Carole.

Pip and Tommy:
> So early? Impossible!.

Grandma:
> It's her. I told her to come home early because we've got Chinese take-out dinner.

Pip and Tommy:
> Where?

Grandma:
> In the bags I told Tommy to put in the refrigerator. Heat it up, please. I know I'm hungry.

Chapter 16

*This is the room size. This is what fits — how and why.
This is what it costs. This is where we can buy it.*

The Chalk apartment. Carole Chalk has called for a Supreme Family Court session to evaluate Pip's and Tommy's planning projects. Breakfast is on.

Carole:
Pip, you did a super job on those pancakes. M-m-m good! Tasty as can be. How were your four, Tommy?

Tommy:
Delicious, Mom. I could go for another two but I'd better not. This is going to be a big morning for me and I don't want to have a bellyache.

Pip:
Let's go with washing these dishes, Tommy, or you'll get a headache, too. I've got to get ready for the Supreme Family Court session, too, you know.

Carole:
All right, children. Our Supreme Family Court is in session. As you remember, when you started out on your client room projects, I told you that at the end of Grandpa Mike's planning sessions you would present your ideas to me for evaluation and budgeting. And here we are. Let's make ourselves comfortable at the dining room table so you can spread out.

Pip:
Can I say something, Mom?

Carole:
That's the idea of our get-togethers.
 But, of course, you were years younger when we had the last one and might not remember. So just relax and let's talk. Go ahead, honey.

Pip:
Mom, Tommy and I want to thank you for allowing us to get our rooms redone. However, we now know how much things cost and it's a lot more than we ever imagined.

Carole:
> Well, children, that was the purpose of the whole thing. For you to understand what budgeting is all about and how you have to take care of new things and make them last. And it doesn't matter whether it's clothing or furnishings or, someday, a car. As you both know, I also took the planning course with Grandpa Mike, when Dad I were a young married couple, but I was always sorry that I didn't have the opportunity to take it when I was your age. So here we are. And yes, I know what furnishings are worth.

Pip:
> And we also want to you to know, Mom, that if the budget you have in mind just won't work with what we planned, we'll make the changes and not feel bad about it. We're sure Grandpa Mike can help us make the two fit.

Carole:
> OK, we'll see. In the meantime, I want you both to know that Grandpa Mike and I had a lot of telephone conversations about what was going on between the three of you. And I want to tell you that I'm bursting with pride as to how you conducted yourselves with two older people. That's something money cannot buy.
>
> So what do you say we get going with the business on hand before Tommy gets hungry again.

Tommy:
> Mom, you're the greatest. Who's first?

Carole:
> Pip's the oldest. So she should start.

Pip:
> Thanks. Here's the plan for my client's room: The room size, as you see, is 12 feet by 15 feet. I've drawn it on this graph paper where each 1/4″ square represents 6″ or half a foot. You walk into the room on Wall A that's fifteen feet long. The entrance door is in the left hand corner. It measures 30″ wide and swings into the room and up against Wall B, which is the twelve foot wall. That leaves nine and a half feet of working space on Wall B. Since the room is a rectangle, Wall C is parallel to Wall A and also measures fifteen feet. It has a double window in the middle of it, 60″ wide, which leaves five feet on either side. Under the window there is baseboard heating. Turning the corner, Wall D is parallel to Wall B and also twelve feet long. It is solid. Coming back to Wall A, there is a 60″ closet with two sliding doors. It's 30″ from the door. That's it, Mom, for measurements. The electrical wall sockets are shown on each wall and the ceiling has a hanging fixture in the middle.

Carole:
> Very professional, Pip. Any comment, Tommy?

Tommy:
> Nope.

Carole:
> OK, Pip. Carry on.

Pip:
My client has three basic needs: Sleep, storage, study.

For sleep needs she has an iron daybed with arms and a back. It goes in the center of Wall C. For clothes storage she has two 44″ six-drawer dressers, for her lingerie and summer sweaters. One on each side of the daybed. They are finished in brushed, off-white. For book storage she has one 44″ bookcase hutch on the right dresser. For study, on Wall A, she has a 54″ desk and a wooden chair in the right hand corner, with 3 hanging shelves on the wall in front of it. The desk is a small office desk with drawers on both sides. It has a dark, wood-grain finish. That's it for immediate needs, Mom.

Carole:
You've done a good job, Pip. Anything else you'd like to present?

Pip:
Yes, Mom. I also have a list of client wants.

Carole:
The floor is yours.

Pip:
For my client's wants she's chosen a white, oval wicker mirror over the other dresser and a pop-up hi-riser bed under the daybed for a guest. She'd also like a 9′ by 12′ off-white area rug in front of the daybed. Of course, with padding under it so it won't slide. And Grandpa Mike suggested an inexpensive multi-media cart, on wheels, for my CD's. He said to put it on Wall B, closer to my bed, instead of in the study area.

Carole:
Good, Pip. A first class presentation. Now if you have an itemized list of the approximate costs of all the needs and wants I'd like you to give them to me in an envelope and I'll compare it with the list I will make up. Then we'll talk.

Pip:
Thanks for listening, Mom.

Tommy:
Pip, I think you forgot something for your budget. The lighting.

Pip:
Wow! I can't believe myself! It's on the next page. Can I have two more minutes, Mom?

Carole:
Are you kidding? Take all the time you need.

Pip:
Thanks, Mom. These items should have been included in my needs list. For proper lighting my client needs two lamps, not matching. One on the dresser near her pillow for reading and the other on the desk for study. The fixture in the middle of the room is just fine. Thanks a million, Tommy.

Carole:
OK, kids. Do we need a break or should we go right on with your presentation, Tommy?

Tommy:
Please go on, Mom. I'm as nervous as can be. Almost as bad as for the math team tryouts.

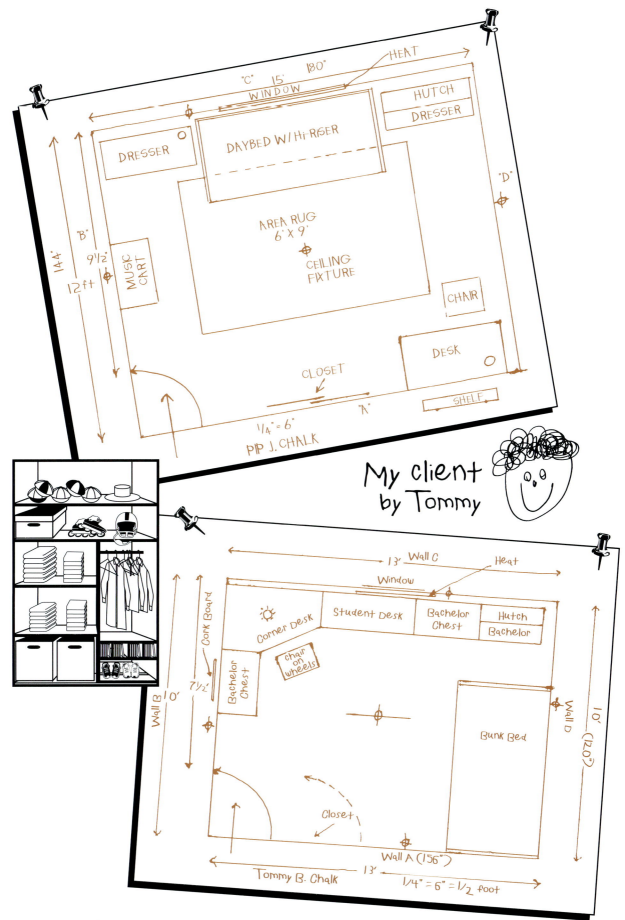

Plans for illustration only. Not to scale.

Carole:
> Take it slow and easy, Tommy. This is not an exam. It's a joint family project and you can't flunk. Believe me. You're on, son.

Tommy:
> I've also drawn my plan on 1/4″ graph paper and each box represents 6″ or half a foot. The room measures 10 feet by 13 feet and you walk into the room on Wall A. That's a 13 foot wall. The door is also in the left corner and swings in against Wall B which is ten feet long. That leaves seven and a half feet of working wall space because the door is two and a half feet wide. You face Wall C when you walk in and that measures 13 feet, too, since it is parallel and the room is a rectangle. Wall C has a two and a half foot window, not including the trim, which is slightly off center. Four and a half feet to the right and five and a half to the left. There also is baseboard heating under the window. Wall D is parallel to Wall B and is also 10 feet long. It is solid. Wall A with the entrance door on it also has a three foot closet door, one foot away, that opens to the right. That leaves a six and a half foot wall. I've marked all the wall sockets and the ceiling has a hanging fixture. The switch for the ceiling fixture is on the right side of the entrance. That's my bare room plan, Mom.

Pip:
> And here is a cool drink for you, Tommy. You earned it.

Carole:
> That was well done, Tommy. I don't know why you were nervous. As Grandpa Mike would say, you sure did your homework. Shall we carry on?

Tommy:
> First of all, my client likes Push-Together-Systems because he particularly likes the corner desks they have. So for sleep needs my client chose a two-level bunk bed to sleep a cousin or two on the bottom bunk. His cousins are little kids. He likes the top bunk. For study needs I was able to accommodate the corner desk and a computer desk next to it on the right side with a desk chair on wheels to roll back and forth.
>
> I planned three bachelor chests with three drawers each. One to the left of the corner desk on Wall B and two to the right of the computer desk on Wall C. There is one small hutch on the chest on Wall B and one on the chest in the corner on Wall C.

Carole:
> Any wants or wishes?

Tommy:
> I still have some needs listed by my client. One is a lamp on the corner desk, with one of those long bending necks that you have on your desk, and two, is a ceiling track in the center instead of the hanging lighting fixture there now.

Carole:
> Again, any wants or wishes?

Tommy:
> No wishes, Mom. Just wall to wall carpeting for a want. And here are my cost estimates.

Carole:
>Come on over here, Tommy. Let the three of us do a long family hug. It's long overdue. A-n-d how about us going to an early movie…a funny one…and eating some things, afterwards, that won't help my diet. Then you kids can do your school work, while I do my homework for the Supreme Family Court report and make some decisions.

Pip and Tommy:
>You mean we'll know tonight?

Carole:
>Maybe. Come on. Let's go.

Tommy:
>Gee! Pip. Now my client is nervous.

Tommy:
>Was that movie supposed to be funny? I think we had a funnier time marching around the mall, eating no-no's and getting our pictures taken together with costumes. Mom, you know, you really looked swell in that large, black hat with the black veil.
>It was a riot!

Pip:
>I think the riot was Tommy trying on the Confederate officer's uniform complete with the sword. I was afraid he'd put a hole in his foot.
>   And how did you like me in that wide brimmed white hat with the black feather and the fuzzy bola wrapped around my neck? Made me feel real elegant.

Carole:
>You looked real elegant. Like Judy Garland walking down New York's Fifth Avenue on Fred Astaire's arm in the movie "Easter Parade." Let's pull the video out, again, next weekend.
>   OK, gang. Let's get that homework done. See you later.

Pip:
>Mom, I don't think you'll be making your decisions tonight. Your son fell asleep at his desk. I think that Confederate sword was too much to handle.

Carole:
>Oh! No! Lucky a weekend has two days. How about the two of us getting into our night gowns and you pulling out Judy Garland and Fred Astaire? That music is still great. TV or no TV. But first let's get Tommy into bed.

Chapter 17

Presentation before the Supreme Family Court.

Next day. The Chalk apartment.

Carole:
  Well, children, if you think you were worried about your presentations you should listen to the grumbles and rumbles going on now in my stomach. And it's strange, since at the hospital I speak to groups of 50 strangers every week. I guess the rumbling is going on because you're my lovable children and I'm afraid I'll make a boo-boo. Besides we're going to talk about money, saving and spending it, and that's not an easy subject.

Pip:
  Would you like a cup of herbal tea, Mom?

Carole:
  No, darling. Thanks. To begin with let me tell you that your presentations were terrific. If your father were here he would have been very proud. Very proud. You understood the client idea and took the project seriously. I know that it will all pay off, in many ways, in your adult life.
   I think, in appreciation, we ought to take Grandpa Mike out for a great Italian meal. He just loves pasta.

Tommy:
  And tuna salad sandwiches on whole wheat, too.

Pip:
  Not toasted. And make sure that Grandma Anita comes, too.

Carole:
  That's an absolute. Grandpa Mike never makes a move without her. Now for the projects. We're going to do both of them and ....

Pip:
  We are? What about the money?

Tommy:
  And what about the budget?

Carole:
  Yes, we are and here's how. I never explained all this to you because you both were very young when Dad passed away seven years ago. But without going into intricate details, Dad, managed, through his engineering company, to leave us an annuity, that's an insurance investment with yearly payments, to see us through if something happened to him. He was a practical planner and worked very hard to protect his family's future. We're not rich but we've been doing just fine, although we can't afford to buy a house.

Pip:

    We don't need a house, Mom. Now with our projects coming along, everything will be nitzy.

Tommy:

    Nitzy?

Pip:

    Oh! That's an expression that came up in class the other day when we read a short story about a girl in the 1930's. It sort of means super.

Carole:

    Now about paying for your projects. I checked your budgets with ones that I worked up and we are a distance apart. However, they can be adjusted to work.

Pip:

    Don't worry, Mom. We can make changes. Grandpa Mike and the two of us talked about how it could be done if we had to. He wanted us to be prepared.

Tommy:

    I can change my two-level bunk bed into a single-level mattress and box spring and get one of those inexpensive beds I saw at Wittnower's Furniture that fold away. Our cousins, Lauren and Alex, are little kids. They'll both fit.

Carole:

    It's not that bad, kids. Let me explain. As you know, your Dad came from a farm family in Iowa. It was a large family and everyone shared in making the place run. And, as you also know, Dad got himself an engineering degree and your aunts, his sisters, became teachers. Education was always a prime family concern.

Tommy:

    Wow! Going to school and working on the farm.

Pip:

    Not much time for clubs and games.

Carole:

    Not much chance for wasting money either. There were two rules in that family. One was, no matter what, you saved some money every week. The other was that you shared your good fortunes with strangers who had less than you did. Strangers who never knew your name. And Dad taught me those principles, too, after we were married.

Pip:

    Is that why we share our birthday parties and give gifts out in the Hope Children's Hospital?

Carole:

    That's why. Now what you don't know is that your Dad bought each one of you a share of corporate stock every year. Good stock. And he never cashed any in or used the profit dividends. He reinvested them. Consequently, you Pip, now have 35 shares, because they also split twice and you, Tommy, have 15 shares because they split once.

Pip:

    What does split mean, Mom?

Carole:
>It means that your shares grew in value and the corporation decided to give all the stockholders, the investors, an extra share for every one they had. Therefore, you collect double dividends when the corporation is profitable and issues them.

Tommy:
>Is that how we're going to pay for the projects, Mom?

Carole:
>No, children. I'd like us to leave them be because Dad set them up for you. He wanted them to be long-term savings. But, what I did do during the last seven years was follow Dad's rule and save a little money every single week because I knew that one day you'd each need a bedroom of your own and furnishings. And by my upgrading my nursing skills, I qualified for a major hospital and that income growth helped along.

Tommy:
>That means you sure did your homework.

Carole:
>I sure did and it's worthwhile for you guys to remember that. Now, let's get down to dollars and doughnuts and then we'll also talk about sharing our good fortunes with someone. Tommy, there are a few spots in your budget that I think can be sliced without doing too much damage. One, I like your idea of using a corner desk in conjunction with a computer desk. However, being that you've pushed them together, you'll have more than ample room for study and computer needs. Therefore, I suggest that you get a less expensive student desk without a built in computer keyboard area. I would also eliminate one bookcase hutch. The one on Wall B which will make your room more airy looking when you walk in. The working wall is only six and a half feet long. And, finally, you can still use the twin mattress you now own for the bottom bunk since it won't get that much wear. We'll just put a platform board under it. How does that sound to you, son?

Tommy:
>Wonderful! I thought I was going to lose my bunk bed, Mom.

Carole:
>It's a deal, then. How did that all sound to you, Pip?

Pip:
>I think that was an easy compromise, Mom. But how about adding an inexpensive cork bulletin board where the hutch was going?

Carole:
>I should have thought of that. Good. Now here are my thoughts for your project, Pip. All your client's needs are OK. But I'd like to see the office desk you've chosen before final budget approval. The difference in cost on that item alone can provide the daybed hi-riser. You, too, can use your present mattress on the bottom. And I think that a 6′ x 9′ area rug will be sufficient and the savings can give you full-length mirrors on your closet doors. Wouldn't that be nitzy?

Pip:
>Mirrors on the closet doors? That's really nitzy!

Carole:
> One more thing children. Are you happy? Good. Then how much do you think we should donate to a worthwhile cause on this happy occasion of yours?

Pip:
> The value of one of my dresser lamps.

Tommy:
> The value of my track lighting.

Pip:
> And, Mom, since this whole project of ours is for better living, why don't we make our contributions to Habitat for Humanity?

Tommy:
> Great! Pip! Count me in.

Carole:
> Your father would be unbelievably proud of you. Come on over here and let's do a doubly long family hug. We'll include Dad in, too.

answers

Below are the answers to the "A picture says a thousand words…" game on pages 98-99.

A-22, B-13, C-28, D-5, E-6, F-17, G-8, H-1, I-7, J-12, K-4A/B/C, L-25, M-30, N-27, O-26, P-11, Q-23, R-19, S-20, T-9, U-2, V-31, W-32, X-3, Y-10, Z-15, AA-24, BB-29, CC-14A/B, DD-21, EE-18, FF-16, GG-33

Chapter 18

*Grandpa Mike's Graduation Speech.
Earning money can be fun too.*

Dear Pip and Tommy:

Dinner the other night at the Portofino pizza-restaurant was just great! It's one of Grandma's and my favorite eating spots because not only is the food delicious and hot, but Dominick and his crew behind the counter know every customer by first name and make you feel like family. That's a unique business people skill.

I felt like it was graduation time and I was all set to make a speech but Grandma would have kicked me under the table if I had tried. I'm glad I didn't because there might have been a few tears shed in the pasta...mine.

Anyway, here are my wrap-up thoughts for two great kids who are my close friends: I know you now realize that interior environment is a huge slice of our lives. After Couch Potato newspaper shopping and several store visits an individual can't help but marvel about the long string of products that you can choose from, even for just one room.

And if you add to that all the needs of the other rooms of a house plus such interior environment areas as schools, theaters, offices, restaurants, medical facilities, transportation vehicles, factories and retail stores you can only imagine the total amount of space planning and manufacturing procedures that take place to fill those needs.

The amount of design, manufacturing, marketing and mind challenges is endless and constantly calls for refreshing, new ideas that make practical sense in function and in dollars and cents. These are idea windows for today's young people with imagination. Young people who want to work hard. It isn't easy. Never was easy and never will be easy.

I hope I have given you an awareness and sensitivity for the beauty of interior environment and, perhaps, even whet your appetite enough to go for it in depth.

One more thing, my friends. One of these fine days not too distant in the future, you are going to have to carve a place for yourself in the business world. It doesn't matter whether you'll want to be a teacher or a carpenter, a physician or an automobile mechanic, the basics are the same.

So-o-o, since you know I have an opinion on almost every subject, here are a few simple guideline hints from Grandpa Mike. They might come in handy even for a temporary summer job.

1. Don't ever lose your sense of humor.

2. Keep sharpening your reading, writing and arithmetic skills.

3. When you set out on your early employment journey, keep in mind that the money paid (unless absolutely ridiculous) is not the most important factor. What you can learn is. Students battle for intern training positions that pay zilch...nothing. And when you do undertake a job, no matter how simple, do your best because someone, somewhere is always taking note of you. And it's a very small world.

4. Remember that a sincere "please" a "thank you, " and a smile help open the tightest doors and keep them open. They also are entré to any country and any language. A-n-d a choice of the right music does magical wonders.

5. And, no matter how old you'll be, still keep your eyes "open." Because one day some "star personality" might suggest something that is absolutely opposite to what your parents have taught you. When you hear it don't say "OK." Instead, go home and think about what you've been told and what you learned in your home. Then make your decision. Because, believe it or not, that "star personality" after lecturing in the daytime, also goes to an italian pizza-restaurant at night and eats ordinary, old-fashioned pasta with marinara sauce just like we all did the other night.

   Luv ya two. Kiss Mom for Grandma and me.

   Grandpa Mike

P.S. Mom told me all about your session at the Supreme Family Court. Awesome! Your family tradition of giving when you're getting is a beautiful one. In fact, an ancient sage once wrote: "When you save one person you save the world, especially if it's a person you've never met and who doesn't know you."

questions to explore

a. What is the Delaware Water Gap? Where is it?

b. What is a "Generation Gap"? Why is there one?

Dear Grandpa Mike:

    Enclosed is my new poem "Jenni's Prayer" signed with my new poetess signature: "Pip Jenni Chalk." I sent it to my pen pal in Bosnia. I hope you set it to music as you said you might.

    Thanks for everything. I luv ya!

        Pip

"Jenni's Prayer" by Pip Jenni Chalk

When you wish good things for yourself, that's a hope.
When you wish good things for others, that's a prayer.*

The stars in the heaven divine
shine brightly for your world and mine.
Our God made them equal for all lands and all people —
they're ours till the end of time.

Tomorrow your song will be new.
Tomorrow your hopes will come through.
Tomorrow, tomorrow when you greet tomorrow
your world will be safe and true.

Reach high my distant one.
Don't sigh my wistful one.
Tomorrow still follows today.

Be strong, my precious friend.
Don't long my dearest friend.
Tomorrow will open the way.

Tomorrow I'll be there for you.
Tomorrow your dreams will come true.
Tomorrow, tomorrow your tear and my sorrow
will vanish when I hold you.

* *Editor's note:* "Jenni's Prayer" has been set to music.

Grandpa Mike's "What is it?" Glossary
Some things a Spatial Planner's client might ask…

SKU's *(stock keeping units)* The number of different pieces in a casegoods collection

C.O.M. *(customer's own material)* Fabric supplied by the customer to the manufacturer.

Warehouse Bar Coding Box of black, vertical, parallel lines in varying lengths and widths that can be computer scanned for cost, identification, location, customer name and receiving data.

Hand-Tied Coil Coil on the base of a sofa or chair that is tied down with knots to adjust firmness. It can be re-tied again when it loosens up with wear.

RTA *(ready-to-assemble)* Parts that can be joined together with screws, bolts or pegs to form a piece of furniture.

Mama & Papa Retail Stores Stores of all sizes owned and managed by individuals. Usually Grandpa Mike's buddies.

Touch-up Skillful repair of wood or mica furniture that has been damaged.

Leveling Adjustment of levelers on the bottom of furniture to compensate for uneven floors and walls.

Installation Attachment of cabinets, shelves or window treatments to walls.

Inventory A list of finished products and components.

Accessories or Wall Decor Mirrors, pictures, lighting, vases or candy dishes for Grandpa Mike's chocolates.

Fitted Bottom Sheet Bed sheet with elastic corners that snap over the corners of a mattress. Don't bend the mattress corners when trying to put them on.

Top Sheet Loose bed sheet that you tuck the front corners of in neatly and fold back the top so you can slide into bed.

QC *(quality control)* The art of making things work and last longer. Training is an essential tool.

Sleep Pillows Those you rest your head on

Toss Pillows Colorful ones you "toss" on sofas and chairs to add excitement and color. Don't toss them on the floor.

Motion Furniture Chairs, loveseats and sofas that can be made to recline by use of a lever or body pressure.

Stacking Racks Heavy metal shelves in warehouses that furniture can be stacked on and are attached to floor-to-ceiling columns. Some are as high as 45 feet and stock pieces are raised by a "cherry picker" with a platform that rides up. Wow-e-e!

Overhead The yearly cost of running a business.

CAD *(computer assisted design)* Software used by a designer to create three dimensional furniture drawings of parts. Some furniture manufacturing plants also have :

CAM *(computer assisted manufacturing)* which can transfer these images to a computerized woodworking machine for manufacture.

Quilting Machine stitching padding to fabric in a set pattern.

Hand-guided Quilting Stitching padding to a print fabric by following the outline design with a sewing machine.

Feng Shui *(Pronounced "fung shway")* An ancient Chinese philosophy for harmony in furniture placement. Try the "What is it?" question on a friend.

Hope Chests Decorated trunks for storing "treasures" in a bedroom. They're beautiful when done right. You can also sit on them to put your shoes on.

Confirmation A written, signed notification of a previous verbal order.

Leather The hide of an adult animal (mainly cattle) that has been chemically treated. Used in upholstery.

Independent Rep A self-employed representative of a manufacturer.

Grandpa Mike An adorable genius!

"Little" People Who Are Ten Feet Tall
Make the World of Interior Environment Spin

Dear Pip and Tommy:

As you know, during the half century that I've wandered around the home furnishings industry, I've met hundreds of people who "can do." "Can do" to make themselves proud and to make other people — most of whom they'll never see — happy. Every day, there are thousands of such people putting together, piece by piece, our world of interior environment. I call them "little people who are ten feet tall."

And it occurred to me, the other wonderful evening when we were all together, that I never told you how many of these folks found their way to home furnishings at a very early age and on different pathways. I wanted to point out that this industry has nooks and crannies in which young talent "can do" if they will it and work at it. Like…

Ricardo Durazo • *Los Angeles, California* • *manufacturing*

At the age of 16, when other boys were learning how to pass a football, Ricardo Durazo was learning how to become an upholstery surgeon.

An upholstery surgeon? Right. In a tiny Mexican town, right over the border from Douglas, Arizona, he was taught how to shape up the insides of a chair or sofa. Years ago, most people had upholstery that could be retied (tightened up) and recovered with new fabric. He became an expert at it.

At age 22, Ricardo was hired as a manager of a 100 person factory in California, but he always wanted a plant of his own. So, he saved his money and, within a few years, opened a tiny 500 square foot plant. Today, he has over 100 highly trained technicians, using the upholstery arts that he learned as a young man, in a plant of 86,000 square feet.

His sofa, chairs and beds feature carved wood frames, leather upholstery and covers (slipcovers) that can be removed for washing. Ricardo's designs are sold in some of the finest stores in the country.

Muchas suerte, amigo. Good luck, my friend.

Ellis Abramson • *Rockville Centre, New York* • *contract window installations*

Ellis has loved cars since high school. His collection includes such styles as a 1929 Model A Ford, a 1965 red Corvette and a 1996 Dodge Viper. Not only that, but he makes them run too, because he inherited "talented hands" from his mother, who is a whiz sewing machine operator and his father who can repair anything that spins in their custom drapery and bedspread shop. Starting at age 15, Ellis was taught how to use and maintain all the plant machinery. Ellis loved the mechanics of it.

A major segment of the home furnishings industry is "hotel contract" work. Ellis worked long hours and became an expert at measuring and installing draperies on the heavy-duty drapery tracks they ride on in hotels. A minor measurement error can be costly since quality aluminum drapery hardware is now available with expensive remote controls that can automatically close or open heavy draperies when the sun comes up or goes down.

Ellis, now 32, speaks Spanish and he and his team travel all over the world. They have measured and completed installations in countries stretching from South America to Turkey to Guam to Switzerland to Germany to Las Vegas and Atlantic City in the United States. The team also upholsters walls and installs upholstered headboards.

All of which proves that "talented hands," when combined with reading, writing and arithmetic can insure personal success. Bravo Ellis!

More "Little" People Who Are Ten Feet Tall
And Make the World of Interior Design Spin

Stan Stein • Lake Worth, Florida • interior designing

When Stan was 9 years old, his father lifted him up on a wooden crate and taught him how to retie a box spring, to properly support a mattress. The box spring is built with individual coil springs stapled down on a wooden base and tied with heavy, waxed cord (horizontally, vertically, diagonally) and knotted eight times on the top of the coil, then pulled down tight and tacked to the base. When it loosens in 10 or 15 years it can be retied once again.

His father sewed new covers for the box springs and Stan tacked them down with tacks held in his mouth and pushed out with his tongue onto a magnetized tack hammer. Today, upholsterers use high-pressure staple guns.

Stan created watercolor paintings and charcoal drawings and, after high school, earned a Certificate in Interior Design at the Parsons School. After Army service and two decades of retail furniture management, Stan, with his wife, headed for Florida with the hope of becoming a full-time interior designer, able to create "dreams" for his clients.

It worked with hard work. Within a few years, his reputation for imaginative interiors was recognized on both coasts of Florida, in New York and in New Jersey. Challenging assignments included a country club, a 135-foot custom ship and a unique Southwestern themed home for which the client flew him to New Mexico just to select authentic accessories.

Stan continues to create client dreams and "becomes a member of their family" while doing so. But, his "greatest thrill" is when seasoned upholsterers ask… Where did you learn all about the "insides" of upholstery? And he then tells his story of the 9 year old kid standing on a wooden crate with a mouthful of upholstery tacks.

Bob Timberlake • Lexington, North Carolina • artist, designer, collector

Bob is an exception. Bob didn't find home furnishings. Bob was born with it in his blood. He built homes when he was 10 and built furniture when he was 12. At 16 he helped out in the family's furniture store and had already won an Industrial Arts Award from the Ford Motor Company Foundation for a Pennsylvania Dutch dowry (hope) chest that he built and decorated while in high school.

Bob loves the beauty that surrounds him in North Carolina, where he was born and lives. The ever-changing colors of the trees and lakes have filled his mind's eye with the natural phenomena of seasons. As a boy he lived on a lake and in the hot summers and cold winters he bathed in it. It was as if he were part of it and it was part of him.

After college Bob became deeply involved in the family business. To relax he started painting with watercolors and tempera. And then it happened: All the colors of nature and details of the surrounding countryside that he had absorbed poured out onto his paintings. He loved what he saw. And so did neighbors and art experts.

Today, Bob Timberlake is one of America's most famous and collected artists, creating for posterity the natural landscapes and grizzly barns of the disappearing countryside that he loves.

Where's the home furnishings connection? In the Bob Timberlake Gallery in Lexington. It is a magnificent two-story building in which Bob chose the timber and brick to enhance his "character of nature" furniture, home textiles and the accessories he licenses.

Bob took me to see that 15,000 square foot gallery, while under construction, and as he rubbed his hand over one of the selected timbers he said to me: "Michael, just look at this beauty!" He was pointing to the art of creation.

Photo Credits

American Drew
 page 99 (#1-curio cabinet, #8-cherry desk)

Appalachian Hardwood Manufacturers, Inc.
 page iii (lumber photos)

Ashley Companies
 page 88 (wood bedroom setting); page 91 (white leather setting); page 98 (#19-slatted bed frame, #20-dining room)

Beacon Hill
 page 92 (bird cage, group of fabrics); page 98 (#12-fabric swatches)

Box Props
 page 99 (#26-simulated computer props)

Bush Industries
 page 86 (pine desk group); page 87 (audio cart); page 98 (#4-box RTA/parts/audio cart, #25-home entertainment)

Century Furniture Industries
 page iii (armoire); page iv (bedroom); page 83 (nail heads); page 89 (sleigh bed); page 90 (room setting, water hyacinth chair, braiding, nail heads); page 91 (leather chair, water hyacinth chair, credenza); page 98 (#11-bombe armoire); page 99 (#11-TV armoire)

Classic Gallery Group
 page 83 (benches, ottoman); page 89 (wood finishes); page 90 (swivel sofa, sewing, frame, upholstering); page 91 (sofa back); page 98 (#18-skirt styles)

Cotton Incorporated
 page iv (cotton photos); page 93 (manufacturing photos)

Fashion Beds
 page 84 (wicker daybed, steel daybed); page 89 (canopy beds)

I.D. Kids
 page 84 (mica bed, mica captain's bed); page 86 (shelf unit, wall system); page 87 (room setting); page 98 (#32-factory, #31-desk)

King Koil Sleep Products
 page 31 (mattress and foundation); pages 94-95 (all photos and illustrations); page 98 (#22-spring coil)

Lea
 page 86 (pine room setting); page 98 (#27-captain's bed)

Legend
 page 99 (#33-computer desk with hutch)

Leggett & Platt Incorporated
 page 32 (bed frame); page 90 (recliner, mechanism, sofa cutaway, sofa bed); page 98 (#3-sofa bed, #14-roll-away bed, #15-rug/padding, #21-bed frame, #24 - hi-riser frame; page 99 (#10-wing chair frame)

Malden Mills
 page 93 (chair, swirl of fabrics)

MGM Transport Corporation
 page 99 (#7-logo); page 100 (truck)

Noble Games
 page 83 (cribbage board); page 99 (#16-chess set)

North Carolina Museum of History
 pages 96-97 (all photos)

Pennsylvania House
 page 88 (secretary, bureau w/mirror); page 89 (gentleman's chest); page 99 (#30-pedestals)

Powell Incorporated
 page 85 (iron bunkbed, iron daybed, iron futon, wood futon); page 86 (jewelry chest cheval mirror); page 88 (trellis bed); page 99 (#6-cheval mirror, #17-iron bench)

Stanley Furniture Company
 page 8 (chest, armoire); page 23 (desk); page 39 (bed); page 83 (bed); page 84 (loft bed, canopy bed); page 85 (loft bed, captain's bed); page 86 (white corner wrap); page 87 (wall study unit, computer desk, drop-lid chest, lingerie chest); page 98 (#13-vanity); page 99 (#2-armoire, #9-mirror)

THE Chair Company
 page 91 (gliders); page 98 (#5-glider recliner)

Waverly Fabrics
 page 83 (fabric swatch); page 88 (bedroom-fabric); page 91 (room setting checkered); page 92 (bedroom, 3 floral fabric swatches); page 93 (living room setting); page 98 (#28-fabric swatch); page 99 (#29-window treatments)

THE WORLD OF
INTERIOR ENVIRONMENT

according to Grandpa Mike

the population: 5,902,111,413

THE IDEAS...

THE CREATIONS...

sleep needs

▲ Loft bed
upper level . . . . sleep one
lower level . . . . sleep one
bottom level . . . . storage (2 drawers)

◀ Trundle bed and bookcase headboard
upper level: sleep one
bottom level: sleep one

▶ Captain's bed
upper level: sleep one
bottom level: storage (4 drawers)

▶ Wicker daybed/ hidden hi-riser
upper level: sleep one
lower level: sleep one

▲ Steel daybed/futon back drop
upper level: sleep one or two

▲ Canopy bed/trundle
upper level: . . . . sleep one
bottom level . . . . sleep one

seek their own levels: upper level lower level bottom level

▲ Iron bunk bed
upper level: .... sleep one
lower level: .... sleep two

Iron daybed/hidden hi-riser
upper level: .... sleep one
bottom level: .. sleep two
▼

▲ Captain's bed
upper level .... sleep one
bottom level ...... storage (4 drawers and a cabinet)

◄ Iron futon bunk bed
upper level: sleep one
lower level: sleep two

Wood futon bunk bed
upper level: .... sleep one
▼ lower level: .... sleep two

▲ Loft bed
upper level .... sleep one
bottom level .... sleep two

FOR STORAGE & STUDY NEEDS
IN SMALL SPACES

◀ Push-Together system with corner bookcase

◀ Drawer/shelf unit with itty bitty sections for itty bitty things

▲ Cheval mirror/jewelry chest
  ★ now you see yourself
  ★ now you see your treasures

▶ One-wall Push-Together system for storage/study

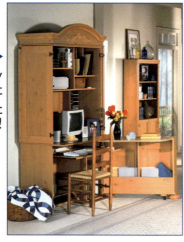

▶ Study wall unit Swings out for action!

▲ Push-Together system with corner desk

86

THINK VERTICAL & PUSH-TOGETHER SYSTEMS

▶ Audio cart
A neat idea — very neat

▲ Six feet of storage and study

Computer desk/ attached hutch ▼

closed　　open

▲ Lingerie chest
Secret mirror and compartment

Platform bed with up-up and out-of-the-way ▼ storage

closed　　open

▲ Storage chest/drop-lid desk

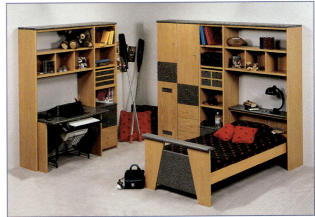

PUT TWO STARS TOGETHER &

Reeded, ribboned poster bed with marble patterned tops on storage pieces ▼

▲ Trellis bed with seafoam finish

▶ Sunburst mirror

▶ Washington drawer chest with marble top

▶ Antiqued pearl finish drop lid secretary with Belgian rope trim

Upholstered headboard ▼ with skirted table

LIGHT A NEW Eclectic ONE

Contemporary flat-top canopy bed ▼

Sleigh bed with button tufted leather ▶

Iron bed with crown canopy ▼

Wood Finishes ▶
1. pickled pine
2. washed oak
3. classic malt
4. antique ash
5. weathered oak
6. brown mahogany
7. classic fruitwood
8. antique walnut
9. classic walnut

◀ 6-drawer Gentleman's chest

Cabinet

closed

open

Relax or sit up &

Water hyacinth chair
Ottoman

▲ Upholstered sofa, chair and wood frame pull-up chair on Oriental rug

▲ Swivel sofa and how it works

Braided trim

Nailhead trims

A sofa and how it is made

▲ Recliner wing chair ▲ and how it moves

The inside and outside of a sofa ▶

Sofabed opened — without mattress

TAKE NOTICE…

▲ Tufted leather wing chair

▲ Ottoman

▲ Leather sofa and loveseat/ iron base tables

▲ Chair and loveseat glider rockers

◀ Water hyacinth arm chair

▲ Oriental credenza/wall shelves

▲ Upholstered sofa (checkered)/upholstered chairs (print and striped)

▼ Upholstery backs count too!

COLORS, PATTERNS, TEXTURES...

Pastoral Plaid
- comforter (reverse)
- shams

Glorious Garden
- bed skirt
- shams

Second Spring
- comforter
- shams
- pillows

A - Italian damask stripe
B - Indian silk stripe
C - Italian woven damask
D - American silk taffeta plaid

concept by frierson+mee, inc.
photo by Kenton Robertson

FORM TEXTILE *Designs...*

100% cotton fabric:
- sofa and chair upholstery
- draperies, valances and tie-backs with fringe
- side chair covering
- toss pillows
- wall covering
- skirted table

Spun yarn wound around tubes, ready for fabric forming.

Spools of dyed yarn to be used to produce certain types of fabric.

Pad-batch dying on cotton cloth is similar to printing on paper.

Knitting machines can use 2,500+ needles to make a variety of fabrics.

Chair: 100% mohair from an angora goat

Pillows and draperies of cotton jacquard

A BACK SUPPORTED WHEN YOU LIE DOWN...

- Iron headboard
- Ruffled toss pillows
- Checkered pillow shams
- Checkered comforter
- Quilted innerspring mattress
- Attached pillow top
- Quilted foundation (on metal frame, not shown)

No! No's! About innerspring mattresses
- Don't jump on the bed.
- Don't sit on the edges.
- Don't fold the mattress.
- When transporting the mattress, cushion the edges where it is tied down.
- Turn the mattress by the handles, regularly.
- Don't replace the mattress only. Putting a new mattress on an old foundation is like building a house on sand.
- Don't replace the foundation only if the mattress already shows serious signs of wear. It's a waste of good money.

The human back is not straight up and down. It curves in and out. A properly designed mattress and foundation set helps to properly align the back.

STANDARD BED SIZES

Twin
39"w x 75"l
sleeps one

Full or double
54"w x 75"l
sleeps two

Queen
60"w x 80"l
sleeps two

King
78"w x 80"l
sleeps two

- Sit square in a chair and make sure your back is properly supported.
- Stand erect with shoulders square.
- Lift properly with knees bent.

WILL HELP SUPPORT YOU WHEN YOU'RE STANDING UP

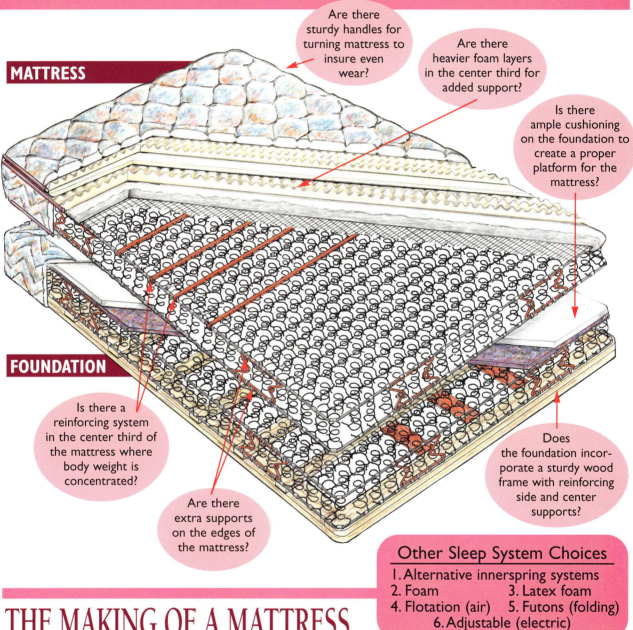

MATTRESS

Are there sturdy handles for turning mattress to insure even wear?

Are there heavier foam layers in the center third for added support?

Is there ample cushioning on the foundation to create a proper platform for the mattress?

FOUNDATION

Is there a reinforcing system in the center third of the mattress where body weight is concentrated?

Are there extra supports on the edges of the mattress?

Does the foundation incorporate a sturdy wood frame with reinforcing side and center supports?

Other Sleep System Choices
1. Alternative innerspring systems
2. Foam
3. Latex foam
4. Flotation (air)
5. Futons (folding)
6. Adjustable (electric)

THE MAKING OF A MATTRESS...

Stapling | Quilting | Sewing | Taping

THE WORLD OF INTERIOR ENVIRONMENT
according to Grandpa Mike

the population: 5,902,111,413

- **SOME HISTORY...**
- **THE LANGUAGE...**
- **THE MANUFACTURING HIGHWAYS...**
- **THE CONSUMER BUYWAYS...**
- **HEADING THAT WAY? TAKE YOUR PASSPORT, MAP AND BAGGAGE**

Thomas Day...

His creations... His neighbors... His furniture legacy of 150 years...

On a recent visit to the Furniture Discovery Center in High Point, North Carolina, I discovered a handsome armoire on exhibit. It was graceful. It was timeless. Dawn Brinson, the director, told me that the armoire was from a reproduction (copy) grouping by Craftique Inc., based on furniture crafted by Thomas Day, a young, free African American master cabinetmaker in Milton, NC, in the period from 1825 to 1860, prior to the Civil War.

I listened and learned that it was another example of a young person in the home furnishings industry who started out from scratch with a dream and climbed his personal mountain to find it. For me, the finishing touch was that it all happened more than 150 years ago.

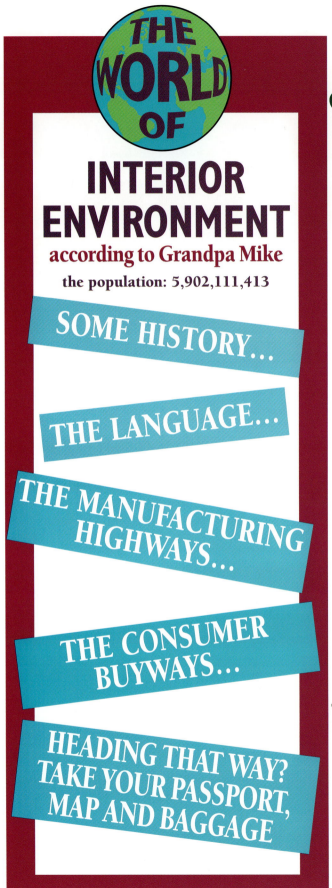

5-drawer single dresser with marble top and swivel mirror

upholstered rocker

Thomas Day, was born in 1801, in Virginia, and was trained as a cabinetmaker at a very young age by his father, John. In 1823, at the age of 22, he moved to Milton, NC, and

AFRICAN AMERICAN CRAFTSMAN

after 25 years of creating fine furniture and establishing a reputation for quality, he was able to acquire the Union Tavern brick building, where he decided to live and work. Today, the building is a National Historic Landmark.

cabinet nightstand with marble top and backboard

Day not only established himself as a fine craftsman of mahogany, but was also considered a fine citizen by the white community of well-to-do tobacco planters who bought his artistic, utilitarian creations.

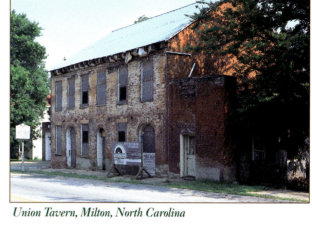
Union Tavern, Milton, North Carolina

Governor David S. Reid, time and again, purchased his classic pieces and one of Day's tables won a prize at the state fair. By 1850 he had as many as twelve employees (even today that's a lot for a custom cabinet shop) and during the next dozen years he started to use power-driven machinery instead of hand tools.

Day built the pews for the Milton Presbyterian Church and was permitted to sit downstairs among Milton's white citizens. Black worshippers had to sit in the balcony. When Day wanted his new wife, Aquilla, a Virginia woman, to join him in North Carolina, these citizens petitioned the State Assembly on his behalf since there was a law that barred free blacks from crossing into the state. Mrs. Day was exempted from the law and came ahead.

In the petition one citizen wrote:

> "*I have known Thomas Day for several years past, and I am free to say that I consider him a free man of color of very fair character, an excellent mechanic, industrious, honest and sober in his habits....*"

Although free blacks enjoyed a higher status than their enslaved brethren, laws passed by the North Carolina General Assembly, as the Civil War approached, restricted their activities. They could not vote, own a gun, send their children to local schools or even defend themselves if attacked by a white man. By 1860, in desperate need because of financial problems exasperated by difficult legislation before the Civil War, Day had to sell his shop and tools. Around 1861, unmarked and unrecorded, Thomas Day died.

fiddlehead banister post

That might have been the end of Thomas Day and recognition of his fine works, but on November 20, 1989 sparks from a leaf fire ignited the Union Tavern and gutted the building. But as Liz Seymour, feature writer, comments, "The disastrous and destructive fire has, in an odd way, brought Day back to life."

Milton citizens formed the Thomas Day House/Union Tavern Restoration, Inc. committee, which had raised, with lots of hard work, more than $300,000 at 1997's end. Everything from selling T-shirts to donations to corporate and trust giving to drives like "adopt-a-door-or-a-window" in memory or honor of a loved one has been programmed. Much more ($200,000) is still needed to properly showcase Day's fine creations. The address? P.O.Box 196, Milton, North Carolina 27305.

Thanks for listening.

Thank you to Patricia Phillips Marshall, Curator of Furnishings and Decorative Arts, North Carolina Museum of History, Raleigh, North Carolina, for her information and patience. And to Eric N. Blevins and D. Kent Thompson for their photography of Day originals at the museum.

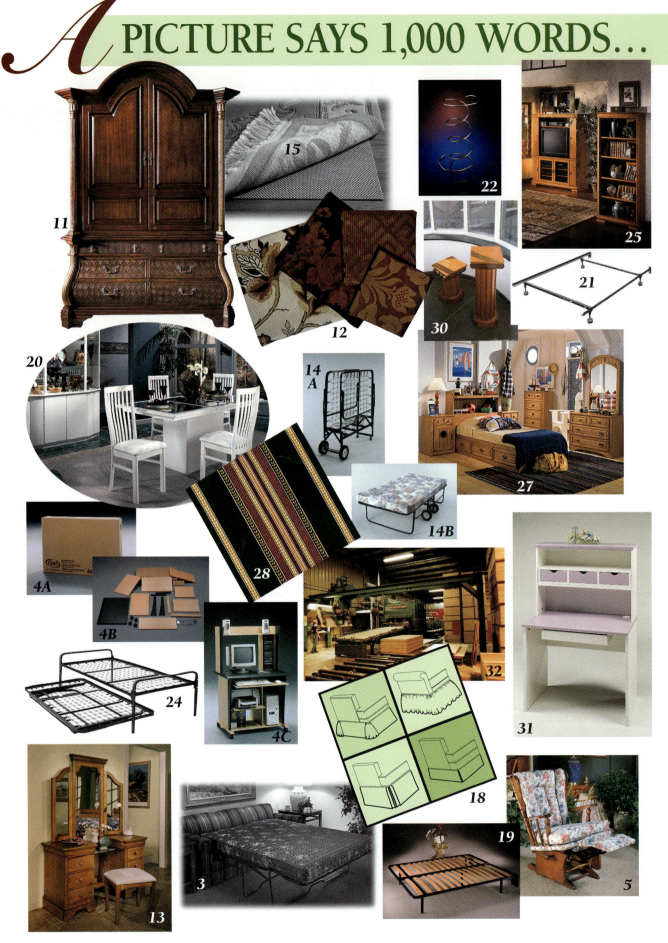

MATCH THE KEY ONES...

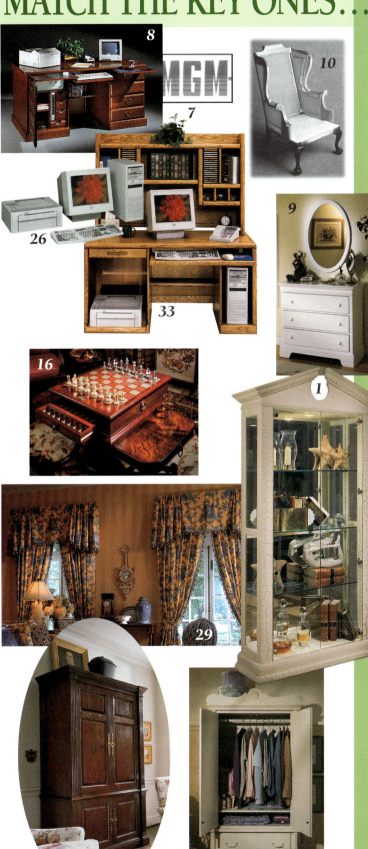

- **A** spring coil from mattress
- **B** vanity w/ 3-way mirror and bench
- **C** striped fabric swatch
- **D** rocker glider chair
- **E** cheval mirror
- **F** iron bench
- **G** cherry executive desk
- **H** curio cabinet
- **I** logo
- **J** print fabric swatches
- **K** RTA (ready to assemble): carton to parts to multi-media cart
- **L** RTA home entertainment unit and bookcase
- **M** column pedestals
- **N** captain's bed with bookcase headboard
- **O** computer desk with props (simulated computer, printer, keyboard, telephone, cd's)
- **P** bombe armoire
- **Q** TV armoire
- **R** slatted spring frame
- **S** dining room group
- **T** oval mirror
- **U** open armoire
- **V** writing desk with hutch
- **W** furniture factory
- **X** open sofabed with mattress
- **Y** unupholstered wing chair frame
- **Z** area rug with under padding
- **AA** hi-riser pop-up bed frame
- **BB** window treatment
- **CC** roll-away bed with and without mattress
- **DD** metal bed frame
- **EE** upholstery skirt styles
- **FF** chess board
- **GG** computer desk with hutch

Answers can be found on page 75

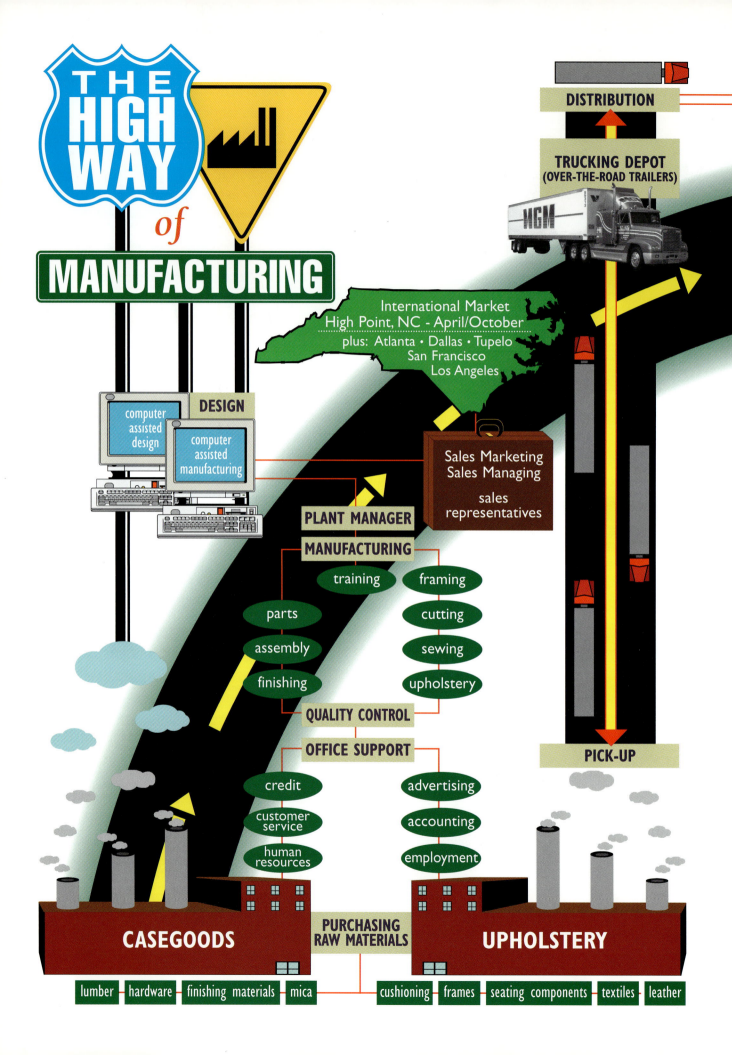

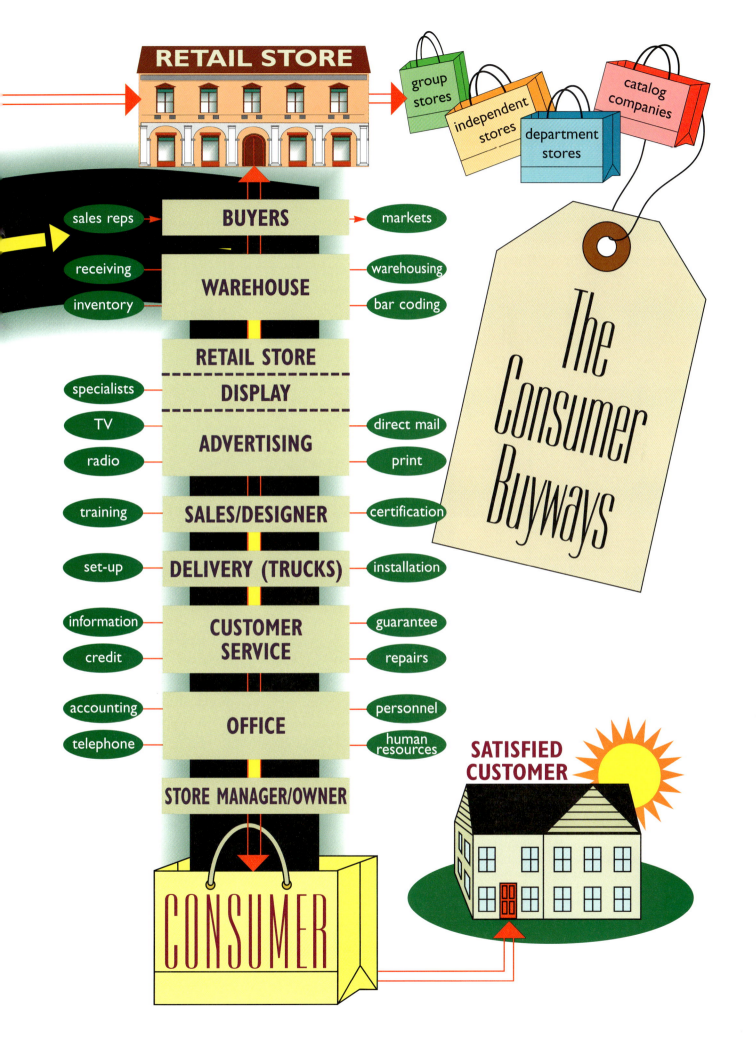

heading for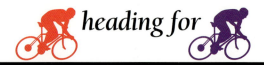

THE MANUFACTURING HIGHWAYS OR THE CONSUMER BUYWAYS?

get ready with:

A PASSPORT: TO GET PAST THE BARRIERS

A MAP: TO KNOW WHERE YOU'RE HEADING

- Study the industry's language
- Know foreign languages for:
  - Import/export
  - Sales at retail
  - Market exhibitor communication
- Study consumer home furnishings buying habits
- Learn about the International Home Furnishings Markets
  - 8 million square feet of display
  - 10,000 attendees from 105 countries
  - 2,300 exhibitors
  - 71,000 (on average) attendees per day

PROPER BAGGAGE: TO LOOK GOOD

- Look neat
- Show up on time for appointments
- Be polite
- Keep your eyes "open"

FRUITFUL HINTS

GET EXPERIENCE HANDLING PEOPLE
- discuss your goals with your teachers and guidance counselor
- try to land an internship in retail store or repair shop
- think summer or part-time job
- accept responsibilities
- write clearly and spell properly
- try customer service
  - one-on-one
  - by telephone

KNOW YOUR SPECIALIZED TALENTS
- woodworking
- installation of furniture and window treatments
- repair of furniture
- computer techniques
- graphics
- photography
- writing skills
- teaching skills - ability to train others

KNOW YOUR MATHEMATICS
- credit:
  - retailer's/customers
  - manufacturer's/customers
  - factoring: the financing of accounts receivable
- bookkeeping
- inventory control
- warehouse locator

HIGH POINT, NC... EDUCATIONAL/TRADE LANDMARKS

- **High Point University** - Montlieu Avenue, 27262
- **Bernice Bienenstock Furniture Library** - 1009 North Main Street, 27262
- **Furniture Discovery Center** - 101 West Green Street, 27260
- **AMFA - American Furniture Manufacturers Association** - P.O. Box HP7, 27261
- **NHFA - National Home Furnishings Association** - 305 West High Street, 27261
- **IHFRA - International Home Furnishings Representative Association** - 209 South Main Street, 27260

★ Tour one of America's most scenic parkways, The Blue Ridge Parkway,
45 miles per hour, no trucks, no billboards, no advertising.
Maintained by the National Park Service.